THE LITURGY TODAY AND TOMORROW

JOSEPH GELINEAU

THE LITURGY TODAY
AND TOMORROW

Translated by Dinah Livingstone

PAULIST PRESS
New York, N.Y./Paramus, N.J.

First published in 1978 by
Darton, Longman & Todd Ltd
89 Lillie Road, London SW6 1UD

© Joseph Gelineau, 1978

ISBN 0−8091−2120−4

Published by Paulist Press
Editorial Office: 1865 Broadway, N.Y., N.Y. 10023
Business Office: Paramus, New Jersey 07652

Printed and bound in Great Britain

CONTENTS

PREFACE

Its publishers asked me for this book. As the task seemed to me vague, pretentious and risky I at first refused. Then I thought it over and decided that there were things to be said about the moment we have reached in the development of liturgical assemblies in the church. I thought I could say something. I thought it might be useful to some of my brothers and colleagues in the clergy and to my brother christians.

In the questions I discuss I give my opinion and take my own risks. Hence the frequent use of the first person. For honesty's sake. I neither claim to announce 'the' truth nor to give a pastoral political programme. Only the people responsible in particular situations can do this. But various hypotheses, perhaps utopias, could enlarge their field of vision.

I use certain data from history and the other human sciences in the service of theology. But I do not regard myself as having written a work of history or sociology. In my 'essay' I take what I need from other disciplines, but do not claim to be an expert in them.

This book is not a methodical exposition of the questions raised. It is selective. The chapters are drawers in which I have arranged what I wanted to say.

References have been reduced to a minimum. There are no notes or bibliography. Not that all the ideas put forward are mine. On the contrary most of them are the result of conversations and an exchange of ideas.

If some formulations shock, my intention was to purify not to corrode, to build not to destroy. I do not want to condemn ways of doing things – and even less people doing them – either in the past or now, but to be a voice within the church I believe to be the servant and spouse of Jesus Christ, animated by his Spirit, and in whom I recognise my mother.

I

YESTERDAY, TODAY AND TOMORROW

No one can say what the christian liturgy will be like in one or two generations' time. But at a guess the changes in the rites of the Roman Catholic Church that have taken place during the last ten years are only the precursors of much deeper changes in the conduct of christian assemblies.

Can we yet see which way things are moving? Can we tell which are the blind alleys in our present endeavours? Can we distinguish from among the profusion of ancient traditions the branches of the tree which should live and grow because they are the ones which bear the true gospel fruits? Can we select judiciously what to prune and what to encourage in the new growth? The aim of this book is to try, at my own risk, to give some sort of answers, although of course they cannot be final, to these questions.

After the long, too long stagnation of liturgical forms, the reform decided on by the Second Vatican Council was the signal to start moving. But waters held back too long and then released sometimes look more like a destructive flood than a necessary irrigation. The tide is the bringer of both life and death. It was high time the church made an effort to adapt, just as every other living body alters. But the change in the liturgy was so sudden and so radical, that it could truly be called a crisis.

Some people think that the reform of the liturgy which is

taking place has already profoundly modified the life of the Roman Catholic church. Others are astonished that it has as yet had so little effect. Rubble has been cleared, walls have been breached, but there is as yet no sign of the new building to house the christian assembly at prayer. A brief look at the past will give us a clearer idea of the present position and the tasks confronting us.

On the eve of the Council, the great structure of the Roman ritual looked as if it could stand firm for centuries to come. At least that is what most of the faithful, both bishops and laity, thought. This liturgy had grown up slowly in the lives of the local churches with their particular usages, it was gradually unified after the Council of Trent throughout the Roman church, it was increasingly hedged in by the prescriptions and prohibitions of the rubricists, ideologically hallowed by the renewal of liturgical piety under Dom Gueranger and St Pius X, kept strictly in line by the publication of only the authorised liturgical books which all conformed to a single model, backed up by the historical work of scholars, commented on by spiritual writers, made familiar to the faithful by the issue of missals for their use. It seemed an impregnable fortress, but there were dangerous cracks in it.

Rubrics blindly followed to the letter, even if they are not understood, even if they clash with common sense, can be kept up for a time by appealing to 'obedience to the church', and because ritual is naturally 'sacred'. But when such practices interfere with prayer and reach a certain degree of absurdity, we finally realise that if the sabbath was made for man and not man for the sabbath, so was ritual made for man and not man for ritual. Once criticism begins to be voiced – whether it be of the eucharistic fast, the seven vestments the bishop must put on or the incomprehensibility of Latin – it is bound to grow. When the Constitution on the liturgy reminds us that liturgy consists of signs which should signify something, each rite must again be related to its meaning. The rubric is no longer absolute. Whole walls begin to crumble. The most spectacular of these was Latin, the language used for all liturgical chant and singing, and thus the body of the service –

words, ceremonial, sight and sound – which gave it its uniformity throughout the Roman church.

Let's make no mistake: translating does not mean saying the same thing in equivalent words. It changes the form. And liturgy is not just information or teaching, whose only importance is its content. It is also symbolic action by means of significant 'forms'. If the forms change, the rite changes. If one element changes the total meaning changes. Think back, if you remember it, to the Latin sung High mass with Gregorian chant. Compare it with the modern post-Vatican II mass. It is not only the words, but also the tunes and even certain actions that are different. In fact it is a different liturgy of the mass. We must say it plainly: the Roman rite as we knew it exists no more. It has gone. Some walls of the structure have fallen, others have been altered; we can look at it as a ruin or as the partial foundation of a new building.

We must not weep over ruins or dream of an historical reconstruction. The liturgical renewal is a sign of the church's will to live – just as the missionary and biblical renewals are. When the poor are dying of hunger because no one breaks the bread of the Word for them, something must be done. When we know what treasures of hope are contained in the liturgy but find that the 'key of knowledge' has been taken away and 'those who were entering hindered' (Lk. 11. 52.), we must open new ways to the sources of life, or we shall be condemned as Jesus condemned the Pharisees. But it would not be right to identify this liturgical renewal with the reform of rites decided on by Vatican II. This reform goes back much further and forward far beyond the conciliar prescriptions. The liturgy is a permanent workshop. The fact that the liturgical rites, after a period of intense creativity (4th–5th centuries), periods of compilation and then of relative stabilisation, finally reached a point of almost complete stagnation, does not mean they have reached the end of their development. Work being done immediately after the imposition of uniformity by the Council of Trent was actually paving the way for the present renewal.

Seventeenth and eighteenth century scholars were rediscovering ancient liturgies and taking an interest in the oriental rites. They were able to see the current Roman rite as a stage, or a particular rather than universal form of the christian cult. It was no longer seen as the most perfect possible or final version. The suitability of whispering the canon of the mass, for example, was discussed. In the nineteenth century people like Dom Gueranger reawakened the essential conviction that it is possible to pray with the liturgical texts, they can be food for faith and contemplation. At the beginning of the twentieth century Dom Lambert Beaudin went a step further: the spiritual riches of the liturgy should not be reserved for an educated élite capable of reading Latin and understanding the meaning of the rites in the light of history. They should be accessible to the whole christian people at Sunday mass. Meanwhile Pius X made it easier for all the faithful to go to communion frequently. Things had come a long way from the 4th Lateran Council (1215), which had tried to cope with the general abstention by imposing on all the baptised the grave obligation of going to communion once a year. Or even from the practice of the devout in more recent times who asked their confessor's permission to take communion once a month or even once a week. It began to be realised that communion was an essential part of the mass and should be made not outside but during mass. The rediscovery began to be made that the eucharist was instituted by Jesus under the sign of a meal.

Another important development was also taking place. Since the Middle Ages the liturgy was an action mainly performed by the clergy, at which the people were spectators. Even the choristers or choir boys had to be attached to the clergy in order to take part in the cult. Slowly the laity re-learned that they were 'fitted for the cult', not simply passive dumb spectators but active participants in the celebration. The symbol of this new awareness was the widespread practice after the thirties of the 'dialogue mass', achieved not without a struggle with the rubricists. In the English speaking world this practice did not grow until much later.

During the thirty years preceding the Council all these seeds were growing. This was the 'liturgical renewal' which Pius XII called 'the Holy Ghost visiting his church'. Although the liturgical law had not changed, every possible way was sought to use the language of the people in the bible readings, to translate these in a manner understood by the people, to involve the people in singing and responses, explain the meaning of the rites and prayers, restore the sacraments to their rightful place at the centre of the liturgy. In France many French hymns which now belong to the repertory of liturgical singing were composed during these years. Again, the English speaking development came later. Without all this activity and long preparation, the Vatican II reform would not have been possible or had any meaning.

The Council fathers admitted that it was necessary to adapt the liturgy to the conditions of our time (Const. Lit. 1). They voted for the Constitution on the liturgy, which was a charter for the reform to come. They obviously did this bearing in mind the current juridical view that the liturgy depends exclusively on the Holy See. However, they also admitted that this reform could entail a diversity of usage in different places and cultures. For this a certain authority was granted to episcopal Conferences (Const. Lit. 39–40). But these divergences from the general norm were to be preceded by controlled experiments which had to be previously centrally authorised. Under these conditions, the immediate reform of the liturgical 'books' could only be undertaken by a commission appointed for the purpose. It was composed of experts and controlled by a council of forty bishops from all over the world. Thereafter it was promulgated for the whole church by the competent authorities.

The experts who prepared the council charter and those who carried out the work of reform had plenty to go on. Several generations of scholars, historians, exegetes, theologians and liturgists had amassed a considerable amount of material. This enabled them to go back to the sources and gave them a comparative study of different rites, so that they were in a better position to understand what the church meant and was trying to do in its liturgy. They could reasonably expect to be able to offer the cream of the liturgical traditions. Moreover the pastoral considerations underlying the liturgical renewal gave them data on the needs and capacities of the faithful today in liturgical life; they wanted to understand, they had a certain taste for simplicity, they expected to be able to participate actively, and they disliked outworn symbolisms. In designing the new rites the experts tried to take these needs into account.

Thus the new missal, the new rituals for the sacraments and the new daily office were successively composed. (It is worth mentioning that the office, sometimes called the official prayer of the church, is normally sung, recited or said by priests and religious, corporately or individually, at intervals throughout the day. It consists largely of psalms, readings from the Old and New Testaments, hymns and prayers. It originates from the practice of the early Jewish Christians.) They were complete services, with full details of the actions and the texts to be used – although there was some choice, which there had never been before. Some would have preferred the promulgation of guide-lines only, which could then be adapted to the circumstances. But a skeleton does not give an idea of a living being. For a liturgical action to be meaningful, it must be complete with all its signs and symbols. Only the mean-minded complain that the bride is too beautiful. How can we regret the unprecedented wealth of the lectionary, the missal or the daily office?

In spite of all these positive aspects and the generally favourable welcome given to this reform by christians throughout the world, the satisfaction, it must be admitted, was not complete. Of course no liturgy will ever be perfect. But we must also realise that the method used – although probably the only possible method at that stage – could not adequately meet all the needs of the case. If a designer was asked to make a universal dress, wearable by every member of the human race, he would either design some ideal outfit which would suit no one, or he would make so many allowances in his pattern that the made-up result would be very different in each case. Or, as the liturgy is intended for groups, if an architect were to draw up plans for a house suitable for any family on earth, he'd have to take into account

14

the type of dwelling, size, materials, style and price required in each particular case, and not be surprised if, when local builders had built according to his specifications, the house did not suit every family.

Of course these are only metaphors. But they can help us imagine on a world-wide scale, even before we consider particular difficulties, the problems a reform drawn up in a central office and imposed by authority on all christian assemblies everywhere, would encounter – what it could and what it could not hope to achieve.

Basically the reform offered structures, elements and pastoral advice. Thus for the mass, we have the overall structure, with the opening rite, the liturgy of the Word, etc. and details for each of these parts. Then there are the elements: the readings, prayers, songs, processions, etc. of which these parts are composed. Finally there are important pointers on the meaning intended by each rite.

But all this does not make a liturgy, that is to say the particular symbolic action of a particular assembly. When we know that a house has three floors, with a living room and kitchen on the ground floor, bedrooms on the first floor and an attic at the top (structure), and that it has tables, beds, chairs, etc. (elements), this does not tell us whether a particular family will like the house, enjoy living in it and feel at home. This all depends on the proportions, style, materials, position, etc. of the house, which may be good or bad.

Even with the same Sunday mass 'programme' according to the Paul VI missal, the service may be very different in different cases. We may say that this is nothing new, that even in the rubricist era there were good and bad services. Of course. But what is new is the relationship between law and life. Until Vatican II the liturgy was just celebrated. Usages were altered, choices made between what was good and what was bad, what seemed to be the best was put together in books and this living practice became law. Christian services had a face whose features could be inferred from the liturgical books. Vatican II reversed the situation. First the books were composed. They gave an indenti-kit portrait of the face of a celebration. But then the prefabricated house had to be made habitable.

What makes a liturgy alive and meaningful is neither its structure nor its elements, but its style, the human behaviour involved. In an oriental liturgy, there are also opening rites, the liturgy of the word with reading and singing, a eucharistic prayer and actions accompanying the Lord's supper. But there is also a particular way of worship, of singing and acting, that is to say of expressing the mystery, that belongs to the east with its own culture and religious feeling. It is striking that people accustomed to a particular liturgy, whether traditional or modern, become most attached to the details that seem insignificant to the liturgical theologian: a particular tune, a way of using incense, the sound of a bell, a particular formulation, etc. When you love a woman, you find her beautiful not because she has a head, arms, a body and legs, but because she has those eyes, those lips and that hair. It is the individuality, the difference that counts.

Obviously the reformed liturgical books could not give the rites a living face and flesh, colour and style. Only particular assemblies can do that. Posture, actions, dance, voice, singing, poetry, music, clothes, images, buildings are the flesh and the face of the liturgy, which can only be embodied in a group in a particular place, time and culture.

All this side of the liturgical reform remains to be done. It is not accessory. It is essential to the 'signs', the symbolism of the service.

It would be a mistake to think it is only a question of revamping christian rites which possess their own inner consistency and permanence, in other words to think that the reformed books give us the substance and the content of the liturgy, simply by allowing individual communities to decide what language, what music, bodily movements and other variations to choose. With symbolic signs, in ritual as in art, form and content are inseparable. The medium is also the message.

It's not that on the one hand we have the reformed books of Vatican II and on the other the task of putting them into practice. When the practice changes, the liturgy itself is no longer saying 'the same thing'. A Latin prayer is not saying the same when it is translated into French or Chinese. A psalm is not saying the same thing when it is sung in Gregorian chant in the manner of Solesmes or swung in the Camerouns' style with dancing. The model is always modified by the local use of it. Even the structures, elements and pastoral intentions in the model are affected.

This makes it all the more important to realise that the model offered by the reform is not neutral. It was composed in a particular cultural context deriving partly from the (mainly Latin) tradition of the church, but a tradition interpreted by a western twentieth century mind, with its own ecclesiastical, bourgeois, scholarly, literary and religious conditioning.

We must therefore expect that if christian rites put down real roots in different cultures, the liturgical expression of the faith and even the faith itself will take on a more individualised expression, style and character. A particular character may be common to a whole cultural region if that region is fairly homogeneous, but it may differ locally if it is a multi-cultural area.

And isn't this the way in which the catholicity of the church is revealed? Isn't it in her liturgy that the church can show that she is neither Jew nor Greek, neither Western, nor Latin alone, but African with the Africans and Chinese with the Chinese?

And what is the church where we are and what can she become?

II

INFLATION–DEVALUATION

Since the beginning of her existence the church has probably never celebrated so many masses and administered so many sacraments as she does today. And contrariwise, christians have probably never had so few other opportunities of showing they belong to the church apart from attendance at liturgical celebrations, Sunday mass in particular. This double phenomenon both gives the liturgy a special importance and, paradoxically, puts it in a critical position. Many of the present problems do not arise primarily from the difficulties with ritual forms, but from the imbalance between gospel and sacrament, christian life and cult. There is nothing to regret in the twentieth century re-discovery of the importance of the liturgy as the core of christian being. But it must be given its proper place in the whole of christian and church life.

As far as we know, the christian assemblies in the early centuries were concerned with the whole life of the local community. The Word was preached. Charity was dispensed. The Lord's supper was celebrated. Even though Luke may have idealised to some extent his picture of the first christian community in Jerusalem (Acts 2. 42–7), it is this totality that is the first thing about it that strikes us. They gathered day by day 'in a single place' and have but 'one heart and one soul'. They devoted themselves to the apostles' teaching and fellowship, to the extent of having all things in common, to the breaking of

18

bread and the prayers. We know very little about what their liturgy was like or even if it was an activity formally distinct from the other activities of the assembly. At any rate the picture is not primarily cultic in the sense that rites and ceremonies were their main concern. First and foremost, before the breaking of bread, before the Lord's supper, described in 1 Cor. 10, comes the proclamation of the Word (for which Paul calls himself a minister, cf. Rom. 15.16) and christian charity (the true cult was to offer onself to God as a living sacrifice, cf. Rom. 12.1.).

A change occurs in the fourth century, with the growth in christian numbers (baptised or catechumens) and the developments in the liturgical cult. Liturgy remains closely bound up with life and close to the people. Its rites accord with the culture of the time. The Word and the service of the poor retain their importance. But the celebration of the liturgy has become an autonomous event. This relative balance does not last long. From the sixth century onwards the people are no longer the chief celebrants. The cenobitic monks stand in for the people in the daily services. Service and ministry become clericalised, the celebration ritualised.

During the Middle Ages – at least in the West, because the eastern churches developed in a different way – the people's devotion was not primarily nourished by the liturgy. Communion became less and less frequent. Monks and choirs performed the ceremonies, while the people remained on the other side of the screen which cut the church in two. The people are christian by birth, nationality and culture. Their religion depended more and more on devotions, customs and usages which today seem to us para-liturgical. The *devotio moderna* involved the devout in prayer, ascesis, charity outside the liturgy. Saying the office and praying were two quite distinct activities.

The modern era inherited this situation. The christian people (or some of them) went to mass on Sunday. But their membership of the church was expressed in very different ways. Christian customs became part of social life.

As society became secularised, these customs expressing

membership of the church began to disappear. Confraternities, pilgrimages, processions and popular devotions gradually dwindled. Religion withdrew to the churches. The rise of Catholic Action did not halt this process. This brings us to the present situation. Apart from better educated, more militant or more devout minorities, who belong to Catholic groups, go on retreats, attend biblical discussion groups, prayer groups, pastoral meetings, liturgical workshops etc., the majority of catholics are only involved personally in the church by their attendance at service: Sunday mass or festivals, the sacraments of baptism and marriage, funerals, and, for some, weekday penitential masses.

Thus the liturgy has become the christian's chief connection with the church. The celebration of mass has been associated for a very long time with preaching on the one hand and community life in its many forms of mutual help on the other.

Since the renewal of liturgical pastoral care there has been a strong reaction to bring liturgy and mission closer together. The conciliar reform put the task of preaching the Word back in first place in the celebration of the liturgy. And for some years various attempts have been made to make the ritual assembly a place of christian and human fellowship. We shall see the problems involved in these endeavours. In fact the general situation has not been much affected. We must ask why. The result is that only a few practising catholics and even fewer occasional mass-goers have the gospel preached to them in the way it should be, or become truly involved as christians in the world.

This reduction of christian life to the cultic element has also been reinforced by the general impoverishment of the forms of the cult itself. Not so long ago even the ordinary christian was familiar with the rosary, the Angelus, the stations of the cross, Corpus Christi and Rogation Day processions, adoration of the Blessed Sacrament, traditional morning and evening prayers, and probably also novenas and other devotions. What remains of all these practices that permeated christian life? Almost nothing.

We may rightly call it not a loss but a gain if christians have at the same time rediscovered the bible, the psalms, the mass, communion, the liturgical seasons, Lent and the Paschal mystery, the value of the sacraments of baptism and marriage. We must give the liturgical renewal credit for having restored the biblical and sacramental sources of the faith. Modern christians can no longer be fed substitutes; they must have the best food.

But in its restoration of what is the very heart of the liturgy – baptism and the eucharist – hasn't the liturgical movement gone further than it meant? By devaluing everything else, hasn't it created the risk of making these banal?

If we look back to a period like the fourth-fifth centuries, when the liturgy seems truly to have been the main source of nourishment for the people's faith, and when other devotions had not yet come into practice, we find a characteristic balance. The eucharist, celebrated by the local church, was a Sunday service. But in many places the people were summoned during the week to a morning or evening service (the office was not yet confined to the clergy and religious). At these services scripture was read and explained, psalms and hymns were sung, prayers were offered for the church's intentions. On certain feast days or anniversaries of martyrs, vigils were held, sometimes with processions.

During the middle ages mass was said daily in chapters and monasteries, and the community also gathered at several other times during the day for the divine office. Moreover, the monks read the scriptures on their own account. In both cases we find that the rhythm of hearing the Word and prayer predominates and the eucharist is a rarer occasion. The situation today is the opposite (except in monasteries). Nearly every time the faithful go to church mass is celebrated, on Sunday and on every day of the week, morning, noon and night, in churches, chapels and people's homes. Proposals for a liturgy of the word, slowly revived for the last twenty years and encouraged by the Constitution on the liturgy, have had but little success. The catholic faithful say: 'How cold!' 'How protestant!' If they can have a mass, they much prefer it. Pleas to restore the office, even in the form of morning and evening prayers adapted for the laity, have gone unheard. There is only the recent phenomenon, not yet wide-spread but important, of 'prayer groups' who gather to hear the Word, and for prayers of various nature and (sometimes) praise. This phenomenon is growing, often in an ecumenical or charismatic form.

Let us note in passing that the reform itself has reinforced this situation by giving precedence to the daily readings in the mass over those in the office. The liturgy of the word in the mass takes priority over every other office. A recent trend has been endorsed and an ancient tradition broken.

We may wonder if this is a healthy situation. A christian should pray every day, and if possible with others. He must constantly hear the Word of God and be converted so that he can adapt his daily life to the demands of the gospel, constantly rediscovered in the Spirit. But sharing the Lord's supper means committing himself to die with Christ and offering himself in the same sacrifice. In order to do this, St Paul reminds the Corinthians, he must use 'discernment', 'examine himself' so as not to eat and drink judgment upon himself (1 Cor. 11. 23–31.). He adds: 'That is why many of you are weak and ill, and some have died.' The eucharist must not become an automatic practice. In order to be fruitful it must have a context and a rhythm of christian life. Moreover, mass by itself, even though it is the culmination of the liturgy, means a considerable impoverishment of the symbolic and ritual forms by which we can welcome the Spirit and draw closer to God.

When they are no longer steadied by the habitual rites of the mass, many christians seem to become paralysed and dumb. Walking, kneeling, raising hands, looking at a statue, hearing the Word at leisure, long silences, singing all kinds of psalms and hymns, repeating formulae, praying for particular intentions, bearing witness to the faith, all these ways of celebrating and praying alone and together become a closed world, a buried treasure. All this could be learnt and practised in other services besides the mass.

It is never a good thing to go to extremes. Jesus warned us against believing that 'heaping up empty phrases' (Mt. 6. 7–9) or a multiplicity of rites (Mt. 23. 23–6) will make God favour us. But 'zealots' always want to add more and more practices. History shows this clearly: more hours in the office, more psalms, more masses, etc. Reformers and true spiritual guides, like Pachomius or Benedict, always reduced, lessened the weight of ritual. Vatican II tried to do the same (Const. Lit. 34). Its success in this was only moderate. We may well ask if it resisted strongly enough ideologies holding: 'the more masses are said, the better God is glorified' or the contract mentality: 'If I do more for God, he will do more for me.' The result is a distortion of what is and must remain a 'sign', of and for the faith. The only true measure is charity. This does not go by the number of cultic signs but by their effect on the heart and sharing in the sacrifice of the crucified and risen Christ.

In a consumer society, which demands action and constantly increasing production, we sometimes get the impression that some christians are inclined to produce and consume the mass in the same way. Others have found that an occasional abstention from rites and even from the sacraments can be salutary if it stimulates a hunger for God, if it revives the fundamental attitude demanded by the gospel: the sense of our poverty. Being rich in rites does not necessarily mean being rich in grace.

III

CHURCHES TOO BIG

Early christian historians estimate that during the period of the early persecutions and martyrs, christian assemblies, nearly always held in towns, consisted of no more than a few dozen people. They met in the house of a christian who could accommodate them. After the Peace of Constantine, the masses gradually joined the church – for the most part as catechumens. Churches began to be built or public buildings converted. Some of the large city churches of the period were capable of containing hundreds or even thousands, like the Constantinian double basilica of Treves, or the old basilica of St Peter in Rome.

As the gospel spread to the rural districts, mainly small churches were built. Most of the small Roman rural churches, of which many remain in France, contained no more than a hundred people. For many centuries christians lived with this double phenomenon: small rural or suburban churches (and convent chapels) where mass was normally said, and the great churches and cathedrals, where they went on pilgrimage, monasteries where they stayed a short time and assembled on special occasions, but where the only permanent staff were the clergy, the choir, or the monks.

With the growth of urbanisation larger and larger churches were built for the ever more densely populated town parishes. The size criterion was the population of the parish. The religious architecture of the Neo-Roman, Neo-Gothic and Neo-Byzantine periods went in for enormous buildings. The prestige of the city, rivalry in spires and a kind of triumphalism were also involved. This trend also influenced certain country districts with large christian populations, and in the nineteenth century the small Roman churches were replaced by new larger ones.

This is the situation we have inherited: perhaps fifty per cent of French practising catholics – I have no statistics but that does not matter here – go to mass in large churches. Sometimes there are fifty or even thirty worshippers marooned in a nave capable of containing hundreds. Sometimes there are a thousand in a church of the same size.

Added to this these great churches seldom contain a single space. They are usually compartmentalised into several naves separated by pillars, choirs, sanctuaries with grilles and holy tables, lateral chapels, transepts, ambulatories, tribunes, etc., even though the rood-screens which formerly cut the church in half have now almost all gone. The Jesuit and the baroque style where everything is centred round one main altar did not produce many churches in France, and there are even fewer modern buildings conceived as a single space.

The influence of this situation on our liturgies is manifold and considerable.

I do not want to spend long on the all too obvious difficulties that arise in trying to set the post-Vatican II liturgy in buildings whose size and spaces had a very different type of liturgy in mind. We need only mention the problems of visibility and acoustics, the pulpits and grilles that need removing. At the very back of the choir there are enormous main-altars in front of which a new altar is erected without finding a very satisfactory place for it. Then there are the superfluous secondary altars that get in the way, the empty seats that fill up the best space, the raised choir stalls and organs completely cut off from the assembly. As well as all this ancient furniture which has now become unsuitable and awkward, there are all the new bits and pieces added to serve the needs of the new liturgy: pulpits, desks, the celebrant's chair, candles, crosses, standing microphones etc., sometimes plonked down just anywhere. It is very difficult to make a new dress from an old one. I know that in some cases the restoration and conversion have been extremely successful and the beauty of the ancient building truly serves the needs of the modern liturgy. But most of us are condemned to the makeshift: trying to re-group as best we can in a building that makes this almost impossible, trying to sing together when the singing cannot be heard, speaking words and making gestures which cannot be heard or seen beyond the transept.

However, these functional and aesthetic difficulties, although serious, do not seem to me to be the most important problem.

One Sunday I go to eleven o'clock mass in a neo-gothic city church. There are several hundred people there. The first thing I see is their backs. The central nave looks as if it is full. I don't want to sit in the side seats because I want to see. I find a place at the back of the nave. I still see people's backs. At the other end of the church I see the disused main altar. In front of it I can just about see the ministers facing the people, but they are very far away. What are they doing? I hear singing. A voice comes over the loudspeakers. It must be the person's I see standing at the microphone. Are the people singing in front of me? Probably. I can't hear. At any rate the people round me are silent. I'd like to sing but I'd feel I was singing solo and making a fool of myself. Now come the readings and the sermon. I hear them through the loudspeakers. But I feel distracted. I make an effort to listen to the sermon. What is being said sounds intelligent but this anonymous voice does not move me. What am I doing there? If I'd stayed at home and watched it on television I would probably have gained more from the sermon. Of course I also want to go to communion. 'We pray you that by sharing in the body and blood of Christ we may be gathered by the Spirit into a single body', as the priest rightly says. I want to commune with God and my brothers. I look about me. Yes, I must believe it! 'In the love of Christ give the sign of peace.' My neighbour does not move. Neither do I because I don't want to embarrass him. I go meekly with the rest of the flock to take communion. But I leave the church feeling uncomfortable.

On the following Sunday I try another church, in a neighbouring district, which I have heard well spoken of. I enter the large square hall with a wooden ceiling. Daylight enters through invisible windows. The floor is sloped and the seats set in a semi-circle. There are about a hundred people. I find a free seat. The woman next to me smiles to show I can sit next to her. I smile at her and sit down. The man on my left says good morning and I return his greeting. I look up. I can see the whole assembly at a glance. Young families, children, older people. They are singing. The leader stands below in the middle of a semi-circle, a few yards away from me. He sings: 'O Lord I come to you . . .' 'And now all together.' Without realising it I find I am singing with everyone else. I have joined in. We also sing the verses. My neighbour shows me the book and the page. When the singing stops, someone says: 'Good morning, brothers, may God's peace and joy be with you!' The celebrant stretches out his arms to us and smiles. He looks friendly. He has a pleasant voice. They don't need a microphone here! How restful. 'Today we have an African priest with us. We shall pray for the church in Africa. And I particularly want to greet the strangers and visitors among you. Has everyone got a seat? The gospel today . . .' After the gospel the priest begins asking people, both children and adults, what they have understood and what they have not understood.

When prayers are offered for special intentions, several members of the assembly mention theirs. Some are very fine. Then some men and women leave their seats and bring the bread and wine to the priest. They stay by the altar. Then they help give out communion. When I leave the church I feel I'd like to meet these people. They are very willing. Everybody chats in the doorway. There is a sort of courtyard with a coffee machine. Some are still discussing the gospel and what a young mother said about it. I think I'll come back here another Sunday.

You may say I have presented my case unfairly with these

two short parables. It is all too easy to describe a boring liturgy in a large church and an interesting liturgy in a small one! Of course. But it remains true that what is possible in an assembly of a hundred to a hundred and fifty people is no longer possible when there are several hundreds. If we really want to make the liturgy work, we must draw the conclusions.

In order to make clear the cases I want to talk about, I will first exclude those I don't want to talk about.

I don't intend to speak here about the 'small group' liturgies, which arise spontaneously and last for a longer or shorter time, meeting on odd occasions during the week as well as on Sundays in different places, halls, flats, churches. The small group has its own proper functions in the local church and its own particular way of functioning. I'll speak about them elsewhere. Here I am thinking of an 'ordinary' assembly, particularly the local Sunday mass, open to all catholics without distinctions of age, sex, class or geographical origin.

I am also taking for granted the importance and validity of the great gatherings that take place on feast days, for special events or pilgrimages, in particular places whether or no the building and site is of historical interest. Later on I shall argue that we do not have enough of these. In such circumstances, most of the problems arising from large numbers or the shape of the building can be overcome because of the special festive enthusiasm of the people. It is an occasion on which a large crowd is acceptable. I repeat, the case I have in mind here is the ordinary service, typically the weekly Sunday parish mass.

Finally I shall exclude for the moment discussion of whether it is either useful or convenient for the church to be reserved exclusively for purposes of the cult, as a visible sign in the city, for the common good of society and culture. Whether or no the building belongs to the State, whether or no it is an historically important building, whether it is used for many purposes or solely for the celebration of the liturgy, I take it for granted that the christian assembly needs a stable meeting place, where it feels at home and which signifies in its own way to them the mysteries that are being celebrated in it.

As for the ordinary Sunday mass for everyone in the neighbourhood, I consider that a smaller building is more suitable to the type of celebration most catholics want today, whether consciously or unconsciously. We can give several reasons for this, to do with the congregation numbers and the building itself.

The most obvious concerns the functioning of the ritual. Communication changes its form when a normal public speaking voice and actions cannot be easily and immediately heard and seen. The meaning of bodily actions, particularly facial expression, is lost. We have only to consider the theatre. The best theatres are not large because none of the audience should be too far away from the actors. (However, theatres increase their audience numbers by seating them on several levels – which would be unsuitable for a liturgical assembly because everybody taking part in it is also an actor in his or her own way.) Of course I realise that today we have microphones to carry the voice as far as we want, and that it is possible to raise the sanctuary high enough for it to be visible by all. But although electronic sound is now part of our equipment and gives the voice fresh possibilities, even in a small assembly, it can never replace direct communication. And in any case, it does not solve the problem of visibility, the personal communication between a celebrant and his congregation when he is so far away that they cannot see what he is 'saying' with gestures or by his facial expression.

Even supposing the sound problem is solved electronically, and visibility is reasonably good, the fact remains that a liturgical celebration is a very complex action. Not only individuals (celebrant, readers, leaders, etc.) but also groups are involved (choir, collection takers, people bringing the bread and wine, etc.), and the whole assembly: singing, dialogues, communion, coming into and leaving church are all part of the action. Anyone responsible for conducting a liturgy knows that the larger the assembly and the building, the more difficult and complicated becomes the smooth running of the occasion. The course of the service must be gone through in all its details with everyone concerned (celebrant, readers, leaders, choir-master, organist, ministers of the offertory and communion, etc.), but we must also realise that all these people involved must be the more technically competent the more the scope for manoeuvre presents difficulties. Many communities can produce nothing like such skilled manpower – starting with a celebrant who is up to the job. Moreover, there are also technical difficulties to be coped with: correct adjustment of each microphone, sound volume of the singing, lighting, organisation of processions, size of objects and ritual gestures. These are questions for specialists, requiring a great deal of care, time, money and people . . . We are quite willing to do all this for a festival.

But is it too much to ask that all this should be done for every Sunday mass? Is it inevitable that the liturgy should be such hard work? How often I've felt that all my energies have been distracted from the essentials of the celebration – the Word, prayer, adoration – for the sake of technicalities! And contrariwise, how restful and liberating for prayer to celebrate in a small assembly, where you can act, speak, sing in an almost domestic way, without carelessness, but without having to worry too much about the functioning of the rites. Then you 'feel' the assembly's reaction, and adjust to it accordingly; whereas in a huge building you may strain and strain without ever getting any feedback.

Let us leave the ministers and turn to the point of view of the assembly itself. In a large church the choir must be raised in order for the celebrant, the pulpit and the altar to be seen. This means that the space in which the priests and laity perform the rites must be partly cut off from the main body of the people. This makes it difficult to avoid giving the impression of a 'clerical' liturgy manipulating the crowd. In celebrating the liturgy is it possible to put across that it is an action in which all take part and that the assembly is the principal 'subject'? There is no point in wanting, saying and explaining this if the facts suggest the opposite. This only increases the unease which many already feel: 'The liturgy is in the hands of the few, the rest of the flock follow (or don't)'.

Various remedies have been tried, for example bringing the

altar as close as possible to the people. The intention is good. But in most churches the result is bad. The altar makes yet another screen. It is the Word – in all its forms – that must reach the assembly (and an altar too far forward sometimes hinders this). The altar needs to be at a certain distance in order to be seen. The action that takes place on it lasts a short time and virtually consists in the eucharistic prayer (the offertory and the communion also involve the assembly). This means the altar should be set far enough back to be seen. A large church also requires distances suited to its own proportions.

On the other hand, even if the small church does not automatically solve all these problems (for example, mass can be celebrated in one in a very 'clerical' way), it at least makes possible a different image of the celebrating assembly. In particular the separation between sanctuary and nave, ministers and people is abolished. Given a certain spirit and a certain style, the whole group can more easily feel that they are 'supporting' the celebration.

In fact the most important difference is neither the functioning of the rites, nor the relationship between the ministers and the people, but the assembly's self-image, which enables them to feel they are all celebrating together. Usually in large churches you only see people's backs and an anonymous crowd. In a well-arranged small church, if the people want to they can see one another, listen to one another, greet one another, talk to one another, welcome the stranger, see the 'differences' and recognise them as such. No one can feel at ease in an assembly of brothers if he does not feel he is recognised for what he is and respected in his individuality: the one who wants to sing and the one who doesn't, the one who wants to go to communion and the one who doesn't, the one who wants to talk and the one who wants to listen, the one who wants to take an active part and the one who wants to pray in silence or even keep himself to himself.

I think many of our liturgies suffer because the assemblies are far too big. This is a problem of which many priests and faithful seem to be oddly unaware. At least, to my surprise, this is what I have often found. I think that in its ordinary liturgy – apart from 'small groups' and large festive assemblies – the church would succeed best in celebrating in spirit and in truth in places where a hundred to a hundred and fifty people could really speak, sing, pray together and break bread, so that each group of believers could truly find its own face and identity.

I've always been struck by the following experience. A new parish is being created. A hut has been built or a temporary place found in which to celebrate for the 'time being'. During this time, which may be months or years, a 'real' church is being built at great expense, which will be bigger and more 'worthy'. At last the day comes when the new church is ready. The service is a disappointment: it's not the same! People don't feel together any more. Something has been lost that can never be regained. What was it?

I don't want to go on to another chapter without mentioning two objections to the pastoral project of making assemblies smaller. The first concerns priest numbers: 'You want smaller assemblies, which means more. This is totally lacking in historical realism at a time when the number of priests is diminishing spectacularly, seminaries are closing down, and parishes are having to be regrouped. If you are talking about Sunday mass, that is the eucharist, where are you going to find the priests?' I simply refuse to put the cart before the horse: ministers are for the people and not vice versa. We shall return to this question. I take it for granted that wherever there is an assembly of the church, it must be provided with the services it needs. If this principle is not applied, this is for extrinsic reasons, which do great harm to the church's life.

Second objection: 'For better or worse, we have the churches we have. Should we abandon them and transfer to various halls? And where are we going to find these halls? If a parish church serves three thousand parishioners at its Sunday masses, according to you we would need at least thirty new halls. This is madness.'

I don't want to re-open here the once hotly debated proposal of my friend Fr. Antoine that the church should hand over to the state and society churches which are 'historical monuments' as part of a common cultural heritage, and go off and celebrate the liturgy in places which suit it better. I admit that I don't think this would always be a bad thing. I think we have too many churches – particularly too many unsuitable churches – and not enough places for a proper christian assembly. At any rate I am not thinking of planning such an operation or of cutting up parishes into little chapels. Many christians are at present satisfied with their large churches and numerous masses. I only want to draw attention to a fact we shall be discussing in the following chapters: most of our large assemblies are unsatisfactory. People will stop coming if they are not offered something else. It is for us to seek and find it.

Finally we should not forget that at the moment there are many assemblies in France which consist only of a few catechism children and old ladies. This is not a problem of churches which are too big but of assemblies that are too small, not a question of liturgy but of the life of the church and general pastoral care.

IV

FACELESS ASSEMBLIES

Suppose we ask a good practising christian the following question: 'Do you think it right that a man or a woman who takes little part in the ordinary practices of the church, but who claims to believe in God, to be interested in the gospel, to want to pray, should come if he or she wishes to our liturgies? Would you accept them?' Generally the answer will be positive, even generous: 'But of course. I'd only be too glad to.' If you then say that there are many such people, most of whom feel repelled from rather than attracted to our liturgies, our good christian will be astonished: 'But nowadays we are much more tolerant and welcoming in the church!'

Thus our assemblies would like to be open and welcoming. But often unwittingly and unwillingly they have become in some ways more off-putting than they used to be. Whereas certain doctrinal and disciplinary barriers have gone, others have arisen of a psychological nature. They no longer merely separate, as they used to, the believer from the unbeliever, the christian from the non-christian, the catholic from the non-catholic. New rifts have appeared between the committed and the uncommitted christian, the practising and the non-practising, progressive and conservative.

But are not these individual positions? How can they affect the fact of a liturgical assembly?

Until recently, although the church appeared to be doctrinally and morally intransigent, its liturgy was 'permissive'. Anyone – as indeed they still can – could go into a church during a service. Inside he saw the performance of a number of 'sacred ceremonies'; he heard songs and prayers in Latin. There was nothing to exclude him, nothing to make him feel out of place. No one asked him anything – except for money when the collection box came round! At most he might feel disturbed by a sermon or ask himself questions about the meaning of the rites.

The liturgical renewal, followed by the Vatican II reform, modified this state of affairs. Now the readings and prayers are said out loud in a way intended to make them as intelligible as possible. They are even amplified over loudspeakers if necessary, so that everyone can hear. The rites are explained. Everybody is invited to regroup. Sometimes you are met at the door. You are given a leaflet or a book and shown to a seat. You are asked to take part, to respond to the prayers and to sing. Thus a full confession of the faith of your baptism is put into your mouth. Moreover, nearly all the catholic services today are masses, that is celebrations of the Lord's Supper. Anyone who takes seriously the words 'Take all of you and eat . . .' and the action – the sharing of the bread – finds it almost impossible to be in the church without going to communion too.

In a way this was what was wanted. We should be pleased that the liturgy is no longer a 'sacred ceremony' full of mystifications, that the congregation is no longer an amorphous mass of spectators, but that they take part in a common act as God's people expressly professing their faith in Christ their Saviour. But this attempt at a new ideal, by avoiding certain pitfalls, may inadvertently fall into others.

Participation in the liturgy has become such a strict requirement that there is now only one 'entry' to our celebrations: for the baptised person who is fully aware of his faith and takes part in all the rites (including communion) and who tries to live a christian life. This means that there are people of various sorts who hesitate and sometimes decide against going to mass in the post-Vatican II situation, for a variety of

35

reasons. It may be a traditional catholic who is accustomed to going to church for feast days (Christmas, Palm Sunday, Easter, Assumption, All Saints) or a catholic who goes to church for the major life events (baptism, first communion, marriage, funeral), who feels 'put out' by the new forms, with an Our Father different from the words he learnt in his catechism, mass with no bell at the major elevation, no *Kyrie eleison*, with new songs and new texts. It may be a young or not so young catholic who has been practising up till now, but who starts questioning his faith in Jesus as Son of God, the resurrection, the eucharist, the church as an institution, and who hesitates to repeat the words that are put into his mouth or to go to communion: ' I don't feel sure enough what it all means.' It may be a catholic who is socially and politically involved, who can no longer tolerate a service which seems unsuited to his militant life-style, not sufficiently down to earth. It may be someone who thinks of himself as an adult and can no longer stand being treated like a sheep or a schoolboy in church, with no right to open his mouth, ask questions, give his opinion, or take part in the group's decisions. Or on the other hand it may be someone who does not feel sure of himself, who would like to remain anonymous among the crowd and is afraid of being put under presssure.

There are also others, who may or may not be baptised, but have always lived with churches and their services going on round them, and would like to know something about religion, prayer, and the meaning of the signs. Books are no longer enough for them, neither are private conversations nor the media. A group of believers might attract them. But will they find what they seek in our assemblies? Will they find it possible to take part all at once in our present liturgies, particularly the mass?

We should also mention children, adolescents, cate-chumens. It is well known that in spite of the efforts made recently to educate people in the faith, most adult baptised people never regularly practise the faith. Why? Do they feel uncomfortable in our assemblies? Even in the most christian families, the adolescents refuse to go to Sunday mass. For most of them this does not necessarily mean they have lost interest in religion or given up their faith, but that they feel allergic to the kind of service which seems both boring and artificial. It's been a long time since anyone has considered the question of the regular attendance of children of catechism age at mass. But now serious teachers and parents are wondering whether this is a desirable state of affairs. Isn't it a bit premature?

Each of these cases should be considered individually. But there is one question which involves them all, the suitability of the present monolithic image of our liturgical assemblies.

We have not said the last word on the subject when we merely recall the 'sound doctrine' that the liturgy, by its very nature, demands people converted to faith in Jesus Christ, sufficiently instructed in their faith to understand the bible, join in the prayers and take part in the sacrament. I have also taught this: 'Teaching the faith should precede the liturgy; it is not the job of the liturgy to catechise.' I still think this is true and that nothing is gained by confusing preaching the gospel as a call to faith, catechises as instruction in the faith, and liturgy as the united celebration of the faith. But preaching the gospel, catechesis and liturgy are not primarily a chronological sequence, isolated stages in the making of a christian – even though christian initiation is progressive, with sacraments to make the milestones. They are not a chronological sequence but components of the life of faith which are constantly in need of completion and harmonisation.

Liturgy is necessary from the beginning of the christian journey and remains necessary till the end. It includes the assembly of believers, the public proclamation of the Word, prayer in common, rites which signify the intervention of God.

Although the distinction between catechesis and liturgy does not fully solve the problem, we have not done enough to integrate them. Our present assemblies may produce a ghetto effect and this raises the question: can one imagine assemblies held in the name of Jesus, where all who feel called can come and be welcome, whatever their level of faith or culture; where they can be recognised in their difference, go at their own pace, as the Holy Ghost and their own capacity allows, as far as they can, within this single assembly, in the profession of the faith, communion in the church and the life of charity?

This may sound difficult. However, it is necessary. And possible. On condition that we accept what I'd like to call different 'entries' and different 'exits' in our assemblies. On condition that the service is conducted in such a way that it does not push the unsure too far or prevent those in the Spirit from going as far as the Spirit leads them.

During the course of its history the church has had to cope with pluralist situations in its assemblies, and has tried various ways of doing so. When the Mediterranean world became christian in the fourth century, the assemblies did in fact have several entrances and exits. There were not only the initiated, fully-fledged christians, who were believers, had been catechised, baptised and were communicants, but also other recognised categories. There were the neophytes, the newly baptised who were given special attention. There were the catechumens, candidates for the next baptism the following Easter who had to undergo intensive doctrinal and moral instruction. There were the ordinary catechumens, who had been marked by the sign of the cross and already belonged to the church in their way but were not yet ready to be considered for baptism. There were the sympathisers who came to see and here the Word. Even among the 'faithful' there were categories of 'penitents' who had been cut off from communion by some grave public sin and were trying to be reconciled, the 'energumens' who were not fit for communion for other complex reasons. They were not rejected from the community; on the contrary they were received and given special care. These different categories went out at particular moments during the celebration, after prayers had been offered for them. Only the faithful communicants remained for the prayer of the 'faithful', the kiss of peace in the Holy Spirit and the Lord's Supper reserved for the 'saints'.

Perhaps the objection will be made that these assemblies were much less open than ours. Were not deacons and deaconesses set at the door to see that no pagans got in? Did they not practise secrecy, the discipline of hiding from strangers and even from catechumens the 'mysteries' of initiation (baptism, confirmation, eucharist)? Were they not exceedingly strict in deciding who should be admitted to the sacraments, even forcing people to change their jobs if they were against christian customs? Weren't they forced to submit to a thorough instruction in the faith? Today we don't hear the deacon call out: 'All catechumens leave now! Let no stranger to the faith remain here!' Could we ask public sinners or psychopaths to come and kneel to receive a blessing and be sent away before the eucharist?

Let us not look to history for ready-made solutions but to help us reflect on our own situation and think up better ways of doing things.

One of the first values to be restored in the assembly should be better connections between life inside and life outside, between the local church and the society within which it lives. Unless a group can show that it is active in the initiation and incorporation of new members it is moribund. If there are only the initiated regularly assembling together and if they are to treat each other always as such, what becomes of initiation? Does it happen somewhere else? It has now become almost normal practice for the process of conversion, the preaching of the gospel to take place not only 'outside' in various 'walks of life', as it normally should, but also 'inside', which is regregrettable. Catechesis is done *ad hoc* within the institutions, both of children and adults. Then the liturgy is assumed to follow for believers who have been instructed in the faith and baptised.

But the reality does not always correspond to this institutional division. The functions of preaching the gospel, instruction in the faith and preparation for initiation (evangelisation, catechesis and catechumenate) are in a critical state. Don't we often find them performed piecemeal by a church struggling for cohesion in a diaspora situation it has not come to terms with? However, small groups are being formed to come together, think and pray more deeply about

God, the gospel and the church. This type of group seems more suited to many people's needs. Doesn't this suggest we should reconsider the function of the liturgical assembly? Should it remain the closed world apart it has become, for practising communicants only? Couldn't it also be the place where men and women who want to come and hear the Word, and share their prayers and hopes, could come and make their way towards full christian faith? We must break down the barriers, come down from our pedestals, stop defending our 'movements' for being cloistered – and often self-cannibalising – whether they are groups like catholic action, catechism or liturgy.

A second value is implied in the hypothesis of an open assembly: the initiatory aspect of the sacraments. By initiation we don't mean a privileged status accorded to the 'full christian' who has 'been saved', but the process of approaching the gift of God in Jesus Christ. This requires faith not as an 'equipment' acquired once and for all but as a constantly deepening relationship. It needs time to make it a way of life. It presupposes a believing community where the risen Christ lives, signals, speaks and acts through other believers. It also needs signs and symbols which take their meaning from all that precedes and anticipates the life of the Kingdom to come.

This being so, the system of christian initiation developed over the centuries which has come down to us seems less and less appropriate today. To offer the total commitment of baptism as fast as possible to the greatest possible number of people, and then force them to live up to all the sacrament implies, has become a dubious practice. It is neither absurd nor invalid in itself and for a long time it was a good idea which could be made to work. But today it poses enormous problems which modern theology and pastoral theology are trying to cope with. Here I mention only the aspects of these that concern the assembly.

First, some facts. With rare exceptions, all the adult members of liturgical assemblies are baptised catholics; they have been to catechism, they are confirmed and have made their first communion. However, many of them, whatever their general educational level, find some essential aspects of the faith obscure and uncertain. According to certain polls, although more than 80% of French catholics say they believe in God, only two-thirds say they believe in the divinity of Christ and only one third in the resurrection. These people can't be called catechumens because they have been baptised. But in their understanding of the faith they are still partly at the 'initiation' stage. What is the faith of baptism that does not confess Christ risen? The result is that the liturgy they are offered, with its bible readings with no time for explanations, and prayers designed for fully-fledged believers, to some extent 'leave them out' and do not give them the chance of a progressive initiation suitable to their state. The bread of the Word that is broken for them is not digestible by them. They are not nourished by it and may even reject it.

For a lesser number – but isn't this a paradox and a serious anomaly? – it is the communion itself that these neo-catechumens find difficult. Some do not go to communion. But what is the point in sharing the Lord's supper, hearing the words: 'Take, all of you and eat . . . Take, all of you and drink', if you neither eat nor drink? Others eat and drink but with an uneasy conscience. Others, more logically, do not go to mass at all, in order to avoid taking part in the eucharist. But if they are interested in the Word and the prayers, why couldn't they attend these without feeling morally obliged to share in the eucharist too? What is the way forward for them?

This brings us back to the need for assemblies with several entries and exits.

If we allow this, it means that we realise that people who wish to join in the assembly are not all at the same point along the road of faith, and they should be offered what can help them best to go further. For some this will be a sense of God and a sense of meaning in their human lives. For others the most important thing will be to know Christ Jesus. For others it will be the mystery of the church and its signs. If it is not possible to find a single form of celebration of the Word to meet all these needs, then we should have several forms. Various solutions can be envisaged.

The assembly could be divided up into groups. One group or one person could explain a bible reading or a mystery; one group could discuss the meaning of a chosen text; another group could listen to the readings of the day, sing the psalm and listen to the sermon. If the means or the people are not available to do this at one service, why not use these different approaches at successive services? One Sunday (or a series of Sundays) the stress could be on catechesis or the explanation of scriptures; another Sunday it could be on discussion and an exchange of views; another could be devoted to the celebration of the Word. Or in a city with several places of worship, or in the country if the people were mobile and could agree on a programme, each place could concentrate on one of these things at a time. It would be made known that such and such an assembly would be using a particular approach to the Word, and everyone would be free to choose the form best suited to his needs. We take it for granted that these groups or assemblies would not only study the Word but also pray and sing together.

There should also be several exits. I mean the possibility of leaving the assembly at a point when you no longer feel in place, without any blame or shame being attached to the person who chooses to do so, or disturbance to the group. This could happen after the liturgy of the Word and before the common prayers if they involve too full a confession of the faith of baptism for some who have not yet reached this stage (hence the usefulness of having some prayers suitable for all, as well, for example certain psalms). The major exit point would be before the eucharist itself. It is just as unsatisfactory morally to oblige someone to attend a eucharist if he does not want to go to communion, as it is to deprive him of every part of the assembly because he does not yet feel up to taking part in the Lord's supper.

If this were put into practice, perhaps various sorts of believers and christians (baptised but in an 'irregular' situation, people seeking their way or in a state of crisis, adolescents rebelling against the religion of their childhood) would have the chance to live by the Word and the signs of the church at prayer, even though they do not at present fully 'belong'. And inversely, the eucharist, instead of being as it is now the ceremony *ad omnia*, would again become the supreme profession and commitment of those who are ready to die and rise again in Christ. Perhaps this would also lead to a new, more meaningful form of christian initiation.

I now want to raise all sorts of objections: Why make all this fuss about Sunday mass? Most people who go are satisfied with it as it is. You'll upset them for nothing. Why not try and meet the particular needs you mention, which concern a minority, in groups and meetings specially designed for them? Your utopian ideas won't make them any readier to come to our assemblies! You seem to make light of the obligation to attend mass every Sunday. You make the Word more important than the eucharist, with your 'exits', which is against everything that has been taught and explained at great length to the faithful, etc.

These are real questions and we should pay attention to them. I could take them one by one and try to give an answer. But if I did this I would be back in a morass of disputes I am trying to get out of here. Let me try to go ahead in seeking a new coherence for 'life in church' today, working out what liturgical assemblies which are truly bearers of the essential values of the Kingdom should look like, in order to convey these values to the people of today.

Our assemblies are faceless because they claim to be open when in fact they are closed, they do not express what they want to. But while arguing that the christian assembly should show its face more clearly both to those within, and to those on the fringe and outside, in seeking a closer connection between the church and the world around it, we do not mean that the church should become indistinguishable from the world? It is faith in Jesus Christ and that alone which gives meaning to the assembly of christians. There is no possible identifiable human group which makes no distinction between those who belong to it and those who do not, those who wish to belong to it and those who do not. In one sense the assembly of christians will always be a people 'apart'. Emptying our signs of

43

their meaning will not give our assemblies the definite features by which they should bear witness to the risen Christ in the world.

V

COMMUNITIES: WHAT COMMUNITIES?

One Sunday evening I was invited to dinner in the suburbs by a young couple who were friends of mine. Because their children were of catechism age, the conversation turned to religious topics. The husband said: 'You're infuriating, you priests. This morning in church the priest told us: You are a community. You should behave as members of a community to one another, bla, bla, bla. They're always going on about community. But they have only to look at us to see that we are not a community. I hardly know any of the people who go to that church. If I go to mass there, it's because it's the nearest church and my kids have to go to catechism class . . .'

There is much truth in this accusation. In sermons and religious literature the word 'community' is bandied about indiscriminately. Many christians who go to church, perhaps the majority, haven't the slightest desire to form themselves into a community. Some don't care. Others suffer. Some say plainly that they can't see the point of liturgies which are in no way an assembly of brothers, and go off to find a warmer group, or else just leave altogether. We should consider in what way the liturgical assembly should be a community and in what way it cannot be.

We should reflect upon the relationship between the christian community and the liturgical assembly. If we are mistaken about this relationship, we run serious risks of

45

dangerous illusions. On the one hand it would be odd if the assembly did not develop community relations among the christians attending it. An invisible communion with no outward manifestations would be illusory. But on the other hand anyone who came to the liturgical assembly hoping to satisfy all his social needs with other believers could be dangerously disappointed.

First let us try to define the terms. In the wider sense we can call communal anything that is common to a certain number of people. Thus we speak of truly communal or community liturgies because all the people involved are, and see that they are, sharing in them. Or we speak of the communal nature of the liturgy because it demands and expects union in faith and charity. At this very general level we could also speak of unity, solidarity, communion.

But community is also a more precise concept designating a definite reality. As the sociologist Jean Remy puts it: 'Normally community implies a territory within which the individual can fulfil his various needs and social aspiration.'[1]

Other social phenomena give us models. The basic community is the family. But the family community, based on strong mutual attachments, is too restricted a model. Only part of the life of its members takes place within it. The village was a major model. Many still think of it as an ideal image of life in society lived in visible proximity and solidarity. But in fact today most people live in towns. Urban life offers many acquaintances and a choice of friends, but also produces frustration from the inevitable depersonalisation of many relationships and the weakening of the sense of belonging.

How is life in church set in human communities, and in what way is it legitimate to speak of christian communities? During the early centuries, amid a pagan society, christian groups in the local church had the characteristics of a sect (restricted groups, election to which was selective; and strong internal cohesion). During the period of christendom secular

---

1. J. Remy: 'Communauté et assemblée liturgique dans une vie sociale en voie d'urbanisation', *La Maison Dieu* (91), 1967, p. 87.

and ecclesiastical society overlapped. The village was the parish. So we can call it a christian community. Urbanisation, with the increased number of parishes in the same city, began to break up this model but still presupposed it. Secularisation brought the major change. The life of the church withdrew or was pushed back from certain sectors of social life. But towns were still split up into parishes; the village model and nostalgia for the parish-as-community remained. Today there is a wide gap between the formal urban parish and the real life of the church. Many baptised persons, in Paris for example, whether practising catholics or not, do not even know what parish they belong to. Parish boundaries are becoming blurred even in the country. People are seeking a new way of belonging to the church in a secularised world. Many people go to mass outside their own parish because they prefer the outlook of a particular priest or group of priests with whom they can identify, particularly in the liturgy.

But amid this break-up of 'christendom' with its territorial communities, one phenomenon remains with astonishing persistence: the liturgical assembly and, in particular, Sunday mass. Numbers are falling and will probably fall still further. But this fall is tiny compared with the statistical predictions made ten years ago. The phenomenon of these assemblies is distinct from that of the territorial christian community. They have different histories.

The christian assembly is made up of individuals who meet at a given place for a limited time and a specific purpose: to celebrate their hope as believers and receive the salvation offered them in Jesus Christ. All the members of the territorial parish never meet together, and on the other hand the liturgy is open to all, wherever they come from. The service is localised but not territorial. Whereas the community is stable, the assembly is mobile: it never assembles the same people. Whereas the community takes a constant interest in the individual's whole life, the assembly only has a visible part in it from time to time.

Moreover, the liturgy by its eschatological rites and symbols attempts to go beyond the actual community. If on the

47

one hand it bears witness to the common hope of those who assemble, it also proclaims communion as something to be created. It denounces the non-unity and non-community of the people assembled at the same time as giving them the sacramental sign of this unity to come. It does not involve itself directly in the details of the daily lives of the christians at the assembly, the material needs for example, reconciliation between quarrellers, the political or social commitments of its members. All this is present but in the form of symbolic action proper to the liturgy. The liturgy gives symbolic signs which each must interpret in his own life. Finally the assembly dissolves and everyone returns to his daily individual and collective life.

Clearly, in these conditions the assembly is not a community in the precise sense of the term. However, it is usually an already existing group which holds these assemblies, calls them at a particular place and time, plans and runs the celebration. And the proclamation of the gospel and the taking of the sacrament inculcate a certain manner of living together according to the demands of the Kingdom. Thus the assembly does not usually exist without a minimum of institutional form and community life.

The need for liturgical assemblies to be supported by some sort of human and christian community life probably explains the uneasiness felt in celebrations which seem to have too little. There is a feeling of lack and frustration. The limitations of the celebration become apparent. How often I have heard comments like this: 'I really don't find it possible to celebrate the eucharist with people I don't know and who seem to take no interest in one another.' 'It is contradictory to go to communion without having anything in common.' 'I can't bear these anonymous masses. I find them a counter-sign of christian life.' Of course such comments reveal an incomplete understanding of the mystery of the liturgical assembly. But they also show disappointed expectations. They explain why some leave assemblies that they find inhuman and unchristian and seek a small group where they can meet and celebrate with people they know. Others venture even further, with hospitality, sharing of goods, social or political commitments undertaken in common. This is rather like the traditional behaviour of the 'religious community', which is in fact the only body that can really be called a 'christian community' today.

Christian faith cannot fill a man's whole life and he cannot live fully in the church, if the only means given him to express his christianity is individual attendance at services. Until a reform takes place in the church so that each christian feels recognised and supported by it, the assembly, the only regular link with the church for a large number of christians, has a vital role. But in order to fulfil it, the assembly must widen its functions and change in various ways.

Firstly, I think our present assemblies are too exclusively cultic. The assembly of the church has never been content with celebrating rites alone, even though the sacraments remain central. If we look at the life of the primitive church we find that its most significant characteristic was the holding of assemblies. The Acts of the Apostles frequently says that they 'were all together in a single place'.

If we inquire what happened at these assemblies we find that they had three main functions. First came 'the teaching of the apostles', that is to say the preaching of the gospel, the proclamation of the Good News about Jesus Christ and the conversion demanded by it. Secondly we find *koinonia*, which we can translate as brotherly love or fellowship, but also as common life. The brothers 'had but one heart and one soul', we are told. This was expressed in practical ways by the sharing of goods and mutual help. Finally came the 'prayers' which were said every day, and the 'breaking of bread', as the Lord's Supper is called here, or the eucharist as it is called later. Thus the assemblies looked after all the needs of the primitive community. We find these three major functions – preaching the gospel, mutual support, and cult (prayer and sacrament) – are all performed in the assemblies; but we do not find assemblies devoted only to one of these functions, the catechetic, the charitable or the liturgical. This all-embracing function of christian assemblies seems to have lasted throughout the period of the church of martyrs.

Later the functions were separated. After the Peace of Constantine the christian assemblies became bigger, with a large proportion of catechumens, which was of course one reason for the change. The services of the diaconate, help for the poor, the sick and prisoners were organised separately. Teaching was still very important. The bishop's first task was to teach. But after the conversion of the barbarians, teaching declined. Gradually the assembly became principally cultic. In a now christian society the assembly was a place where ceremonies were performed by priests. The people were spectators. After the Council of Trent there was a new effort to catechise adults (catechisms, parish missions) and a start was made in the catechising of children, but this was done outside the liturgy. The rubricist era reinforced the split between the sacred rites and every other christian act of piety, teaching or charity. The liturgical reform of this century developed in this cultic context and our Sunday assemblies are still almost exclusively contained within it.

The Vatican II reform began to redress the balance. It strongly stressed the function of the Word in every liturgical assembly. However, proclamation of the Word was thought of in its ritualised form: bible readings and a sermon by the president of the assembly (or at least another priest). It assumed that catechism, and instruction on the bible and theology, were given elsewhere. But it quickly became apparent that the majority of practising christians had no other food of the gospel than their Sunday mass, and that mere readings from the bible and a sermon were not enough for the bread of the Word to be truly broken, given and inwardly digested. Efforts were then made to share the Word in small groups, to have conversational sermons, less difficult non-biblical readings, discussion of texts, to change the strictly ritualised liturgy of the Word into something which would enable everyone to hear and understand the gospel according to his capacity. The assembly is again becoming the place of teaching. We will take up this point again in a chapter of its own.

There remains the function which *Acts* calls *koinonia*. The Vatican II *Ordo missae* (the official handbook giving the structure of the new mass) disposes of it in two words, its first two: *populo congregato*: 'the people having been assembled . . .' That it is to say that it presupposes that the problem has been solved when the liturgy begins. But the question is precisely to know whether the people bodily present – and even their arrival has to cope with the problem of lateness, some as late as the offertory – have human relationships between them which make it possible to hear the word in common in a fruitful manner, really to share their prayers, and brotherly communion. It was probably no accident that *Acts* put *koinonia* before the prayers and the breaking of bread.

The symbolic rites of the liturgy are only meaningful to the extent that the assembly celebrating them gives them meaning. Isn't this what people suffering from the anonymity and lack of fellowship in our assemblies are getting at? 'We don't know each other.' 'We can't even say good morning to each other in church.' The attempts at welcome at the beginning of the assemblies, the mutual introductions in small groups, the coffee after mass are all trying to respond to the basic human need. They are but feeble palliatives for the felt lack of *koinonia*. Clearly, if there is no human communion, the sharing of the Word remains formal, the proposal of intentions for prayers which are rather personal becomes impossible or embarrassing, community as mutual help remains an abstraction.

Finally, if the liturgical assembly does not identify itself with the local christian community, this community will need other ways of asserting its existence. But where are there 'assemblies of the church' – apart from the liturgical – in which questions regarding its life are dealt with? The organisation of the various services, the liturgical, catechetic and charitable; the appointment of people to certain functions; the maintenance of the clergy and their lay helpers; the upkeep and cleaning of the church itself; aid for the poorest, the missions, the Third World; the initiation of children, the place of adolescents, preparation for marriage; investigation of the population of the district and its need for evangelisation, etc: all these pastoral decisions are usually taken by priests with at best the help of some of the most devout or influential lay people. The method of government, whether technocratic or autocratic, does not correspond to the modern and even less to the gospel view of living together.

Shouldn't we now admit the necessity of christian assemblies which are not concerned solely with the hearing of the word and celebrating the eucharist, but also with living together according to the gospel? It has been proposed that every Sunday, at the beginning of the assembly, time is taken to pay attention to the people (present or absent), the better to know to whom the word is addressed and what the sharing of the bread involves. In some places such assemblies are held once or several times during the year. The church is seeking a face so that it may become a community.

If we want to find a better balance of function in a church assembly, so that not only the ritual but also the teaching and community needs are served, in order to put these theories into practice and give substance to the sporadic attempts made here and there, we must look at our assemblies as they really are, their composition, frequency and size. In a large city parish with Sunday masses every hour, how is it possible to share the gospel truly and encourage socialising among christians? And how about the deserted country churches which the priest hastily visits in his small car and finds when he arrives a few minutes before mass eight children and four women? We must look at the reality but not be overwhelmed by it.

In fact our parishes, with their mapped-out territory centred on a church with its clergy and services, are in a manifold state of crisis. We should entirely rethink the institution of the parish. This will need time, and as yet no suitable 'model' institution has been tried and tested. However, the Sunday assemblies take place. They continue to exist and develop, whatever the vicissitudes of the institution of the parish and its ministers. They are, I am convinced, the surest proof of the continuance of a living church whose pastoral and missionary structures are being transformed. Let us try to trace some common characteristics of these assemblies and consider under what conditions they can function. We are thinking here of the regular, local, open assembly. For the sake of brevity we shall call it the 'Sunday' ('dominical') assembly, in the etymological sense of the assembly of the risen 'Lord' – without for the moment being any more precise about its connection with the day of the week we call 'Sunday'.

Firstly, these assemblies are held in a particular, accessible place on a known day at a known time. They are open to all believers (or those who wish to believe) in the God of Jesus Christ. In this sense they are 'public', unlike the small groups. Any 'brother' can come, and finds himself taking part in the service as far as his faith allows, even if he is only passing through. The assemblies usually have a local base. They depend on a heterogeneous core of faithful. There are those who go to the nearest church. There are those who have chosen to go regularly to this particular church. There are, necessarily, the people responsible for the celebration, the priests and ministers who perform various functions. They make the normal connection between the assembly and the local community (whether geographical or not). Thus on the one hand the community holds regular assemblies. On the other it is in the assembly which hears the word and shares the bread that the community of the church is created.

A connection between the Sunday assembly and the local community seems to be indispensable for the proper functioning of the celebration. A core of regulars is needed for the celebration to be held easily: regular services, common language, known songs, group habits. The functioning of the ritual cannot be improvised anew each time; participation would become more difficult and require efforts which would be better employed in listening to the word, in prayer and adoration. The reaction of the group to the signs and symbols offered them is an indication of how these can be interpreted, checked and adjusted. How is it possible to know whether the language used is right, the style of celebration appropriate, the songs and prayers suitable, the general tone proper if there is not at least a core of people who know one another, who have at least a minimum of common life and culture which they can bring to the group? This is even more necessary if we are trying to judge the impact of the Word proclaimed and the validity (not merely juridical but human) of the sacraments.

To give this type of assembly the chance of functioning well I have already spoken of the importance of numbers and size. I do not think that an assembly can at the moment balance the functions of the Word, fraternal charity and ritual if it contains several hundred people. If I am right, this means that this type of ordinary assembly – we have called it the Sunday assembly and it would be the basic cell of the local church – should contain fewer people than in most urban parishes and more than in certain depopulated rural areas.

This also means that we must distinguish two levels of pastoral organisation within a diocese. An intermediate level should cover a fairly large area and be able to provide all the services of a complete and quasi-autonomous local church: preaching the gospel, catechesis, preparation for baptism and marriage, various movements and good works, etc, with a representative of the bishop and a priest's house. The base level would be organised round the Sunday eucharist, and all that concerns the ordinary lives of the people attending it. Strictly speaking only the 'area' would correspond to the christian community, whereas the 'Sunday' assemblies would be sub-communities. Then it would become possible within a particular area for the sub-communities to specialise their Sunday services for particular needs. They would no longer try to do everything like the old self-sufficient parishes. In one place the stress would be on catechesis, in another on discussing contemporary problems of the faith; in one place they could concentrate on the initiation of children or the integration of young people, in another on a more contemplative liturgy, etc. Existing realities would be taken into account, the abilities and gifts of the people available, projects already begun and needs perceived. The christians in the area could thus choose the ordinary assembly that suited them best and change if they wanted to.

This plan also involves another complementary one. If the

church is to live primarily through its local assemblies, three levels of assembly would be necessary. I have already alluded to these three types of assembly. Here I outline them briefly.

First we must realise the importance and usefulness of the small groups of all kinds that have recently arisen spontaneously. They allow for close relationships where each member can be welcomed and recognised in his individuality, according to his own level of faith and culture. They develop a strong sense of belonging (to Christ and to the church through and in the group). Their approach to the gospel is usually serious, demanding and detailed. Common prayers are simple and deep. The eucharists they celebrate come closer to the participants. The symbolism of the shared bread and common cup becomes clearer. The members feel 'involved'. This type of belonging gives some their deepest sense of living in Christ, the gospel and the church. But we should remember that these small groups only ever involve a minority of christians. They are too narrow to offer all the various aspects of life in church and provide a 'base community'. They could not, for example, undertake christian initiation because they lack duration and stability. They give only a partial image of the church. This means they must always be careful to remain open to other communions. They are greenhouses to germinate seedlings for transplanting outside.

At the other extreme, the church needs festival assemblies attended by large crowds at important times and places. The levelling down of feast days by the Council to make them indistinguishable from ordinary Sundays was a serious loss. A festival can show in a special way the great variety of the christian people, consisting of the lame and the blind, white and black, rich and poor, men and women, old people and children whom the Good News invites to the wedding feast. The feast is celebrated in symbols that for once are manifest as such without wavering between ritualism and demystification. It gives some people the opportunity they lack at their Sunday mass to receive help and support in their religion and their faith. I would assimilate into these great festival assemblies the cult normally celebrated in prominent places: cathedrals, basilicas and churches at places of pilgrimage, historic sanctuaries where people from all nations come, speaking all languages, from every walk of life and level of faith. Then there can be no question of 'community'. They are one-off assemblies even if the place of celebration also has its regulars. The liturgy on these occasions needs experts to enable it to function well: clergy, leaders, choir, organist, people at the door. Celebration with a heterogeneous and changing crowd requires, in order to be successful, appropriate technical aids and competent personnel.

Between the more or less spontaneous and selective small groups and the occasional great festival assemblies, the church cannot live without relatively stable local assemblies, normally linked to a territorial community. These assemblies mean primarily God's permanent call to his people to hear his word and celebrate the covenant. The church as God's 'convocation' is primarily in the individual's attendance at the assembly. It should be the chief mark of the weekly convocation on the day which commemorates the resurrection of the Lord and where his coming is made real. It is neither possible nor indispensable that everybody should come to the assembly, although they are all convoked, but it is necessary for the assembly to take place so that God's gift may be offered to all by his church who is its trustee and mediator.

One last practical remark: if an assembly-community needs to redress the balance in its functions of living together in the church, either by laying more stress on personal relations or by intensifying the various forms of transmitting the faith, do we need other assemblies to do this as well as the ordinary assembly which we have called the Sunday assembly? A weekly assembly is in itself quite taxing, given the pace of modern life. It is even too much for some. If we create extra assemblies only a few will come, always the same people: the most committed, the most devout. Most 'practising' catholics will not come to these meetings. They will continue to come on Sundays to 'hear mass'. Thus the Sunday mass will remain as it is. Wouldn't it be wiser to build on what we already have, that is to say our Sunday assembly? This is where we must put *koinonia* into practice with the triple sharing of the Word, goods (not only material goods) and the bread. If the present shape of our mass is too rigid to contain all this we must stretch it. The aim is that the church should live. The church will live if its assemblies are alive.

VI

LIGHT IN DARK TIMES

The festival is both repetition and novelty. Whether it be the
National festival, Mothers' Day or Palm Sunday, there is a
predetermined date on which this feast is celebrated rather
than on any other day during the year. There are rites: dancing and fireworks; presents; the procession with blessed
palms. Nearly all the details of the festival are repeated year
after year. However, if there was the feeling of merely
repeating what had been already done the festival would be
spoilt. The festival is an event. Something is expected to happen: the march and the speech that catalyse political energies;
the special meal for Mothers' Day which heightens family feeling; the palm which, according to how you think of it, recalls
the memory of the dead, guarantees God's protection, introduces Holy Week, bears witness to a Lordship not of this
world.

Every liturgical celebration also shares these two aspects of
the festival. The liturgical renewal revalued the Sunday service as a weekly festival celebrating the Lord's resurrection.
Every 'first day of the week' christians gather in memory of the
first Easter Day. Every week they re-read the gospel and re-
enact the Lord's supper: by these repetitive rites they are
celebrating something 'to come': the coming of the Kingdom.
They welcome in faith the liberation brought to the world by
the Lord's death and resurrection. How far are practising
christians aware of this theology and spirituality of the Sun-

day service? There is a wide gap between theology and practice. There always has been and probably always will be. But what is perhaps new is a kind of weariness which appears in remarks like these: 'You say that the liturgy is a festival, that every Sunday mass is the festival of the risen Christ. But that is not how we find it. Our Sunday masses stink of boredom, we've been through it all so many times, it's a duty. Our assemblies are not at all like a festive gathering. We need a less fixed, more inventive, more joyful liturgy.' And the adjective most often heard is: 'Your liturgies are dreary.'

We could protest that never have such efforts been made to make the celebration interesting and lively, and that never before have the people taken such an active part. Some liturgical teams go to great imaginative lengths to bring out the theme of the day, present the readings, find apt prayer intentions, joyful, popular songs with good rhythms, guitars . . . That's all true. But it seems as if all our great efforts to organise each Sunday festival only make the people feel more tired.

Let us try to sort out the problem without being too ready to take our wishes for reality or our apparent successes for real. A few years ago when the new 'rhythmic songs' took over in our churches, many priests thought that at last the spectre of 'dreary hymns' would be banished from our liturgies, and that the people most concerned, the adolescents and the young, would find mass exciting again. All over the place 'young people's masses' were put on, with percussion, guitar and swung rhythms (sometimes the rhythms were hammered out rather than swung but that didn't matter). This trend lasted a few years and then died down. Everything was not lost. New, more exciting songs had been found. But there are no longer special masses for the young. And thus the question of Sunday mass has become all the more ticklish.

We must make a distinction here. It is correct to say that every christian celebration is by its nature a festival, if by festival we mean the symbolic action by which believers commemorate their paschal liberation in Christ and draw strength from it in the hope of the new world to come. But this is a festival of the spirit that is lived in faith. It is a 'mystical' reality in which the invisible is seen in visible symbolism. The christian's involvement in the paschal mystery cannot be quantified in the amount of visible festivity that goes on in a liturgical celebration. I can go as deeply into the mystery during a home eucharist in which the ritual paraphernalia are reduced to a strict minimum as during a solemn liturgy. That is to say, we must distinguish between the festival of the spirit which is in accordance with the measure of faith and the festive expression of the celebration which depends on the signs and symbols used.

The amount of festivity required is not decided by what is being celebrated, which is always the same salvation offered by God, but by the needs and capacities of the people assembled to celebrate. The criteria here are human, historical, anthropological, cultural and natural, pedagogical and pastoral. These criteria have been responsible for the development of christian festivals and the liturgical cycle, the essentials of which have given the church's face its features. On another level these criteria must also be the guide for christian assemblies in their celebrations.

First point: 'Every day is not a festival.' There is a contrast between the ordinary day and the festival. Festival implies a special day, something extravagant. Time, money and work are put into it. It can only happen on exceptional occasions, important dates or symbolic days. Festivals, however, are as necessary to man as his daily bread. They can give meaning to his life. They signify the 'elsewhere' without which the here and how would make no sense. They signify this new world and make it present.

If this is the case the church, like every other social group, needs festivals in the sense of 'festive occasions' when the mystery is signified in a more intense manner. This is particularly so of the Easter Triduum and Christmas. But what about the Sunday celebration? Or rather what degree of festivity could be given to Sunday mass to make it credible, meaningful and fruitful?

Before going on with this question I'd like to repeat a point I have already made: the post-conciliar liturgical reform is based on a very fine theology of Sunday, the liturgical seasons and festivals, but paradoxically it seems to have produced a levelling down of festivals.

Every pastoral effort has been made to involve the faithful actively in every mass: more bible readings; texts translated and read, often with an introduction and explanation; simplified rites to make them more 'transparent'; simple songs – new for the most part since they have replaced the Latin ones – so that everyone can join in; a more straightforward and familiar style which is less hierarchical and less triumphalist. All this work has been important and the results largely positive. But we should consider all the consequences. It also means the disappearance of chants which had become the symbol of a particular liturgical season or festival (e.g. *Rorate*, *Adeste* . . .); the abandonment of the special ceremonies for a certain day (Corpus Christi, Candlemas and Rogation Day processions; Maundy Thursday exposition, etc.); general dimming of the colour of the liturgical seasons. In other words the celebrations have been levelled down. Today in many parishes there is hardly any difference between Whit Sunday and an ordinary Sunday. Because every Sunday has been made more important, the special days no longer stand out. The reason for this is that true symbols cannot be manufactured, they are produced by a culture. The liturgical reform is less the cause than the sign of this.

It is not the church alone that has lost the symbols necessary to any festival. It is common to our whole society because our culture has broken down. The church's festivals grew up in symbiosis with the socio-religious life of the society in which the gospel was preached. The church took over certain pagan usages – either dates like the Winter solstice on December 25th or spring festivals for the Rogations of St Mark; or ritual elements like presents, Christmas trees, Easter eggs. Then it infused new meaning into these usages. Thus pairs arose like All Saints and All Souls, Christmas and the festival of the family, Lent and Shrove Tuesday (with its counter-festival of the Forty Hours). Apart from Christmas,

61

what remains of this socio-religious framework in our secularised industrialised culture? Holiday dates such as Easter, or holidays which give people extra days off, 'bridges', (Ascension, August 15th, November 1st) with here and there a bit of folklore. But our society no longer has 'sacred seasons' which could offer a basis for our christian celebrations.

Of course we could mention several festivals of modern origin, like May Day or Mothers' Day. But has the Church succeeded in assimilating May Day to a feast of St Joseph the worker? No, it hasn't.

If the church wants festivals, special times of year, she must hold them with and within the community of believers without the support of society in general. Wasn't this also the case for the early church which lived in a pagan society, when the christian Sunday was not related to the civil calendar? The church today may be forced, in order to be able to celebrate its festivals as it wishes, to cut itself off from social customs which it created but which have now turned against it. I am thinking in particular of the date of Easter and the holidays connected with it. In certain city parishes the Easter holidays cause a mass departure of the bulk of the christian community. This means that part of the sense is lost when Lent celebrated together is cut off without ending in a common celebration of the paschal mystery. If the Easter vigil is the greatest of all feasts for christians shouldn't we find a way of celebrating it that suits the community best? Of course I am not suggesting that each community should fix the date of Easter at will, but that human considerations are more important than astronomical in the fixing of it. When christians try to find a common date for Easter between separated churches, we find that the essential is not the 14th Nizan, abandoned since the Second Century, nor the phasing of the moon in that month we have fixed on in our calendar, but the commemoration of the Resurrection which the church celebrates on that day.

On the other hand the church could make use of favourable times in the civil calendar to institute new festivals. Every parish knows that the beginning of the new school year is a crucial moment in the life of the community. It, rather than

January 1st, is the real beginning of the year. Plans are drawn up for the year ahead, pastoral activities start up again, and on their return from their holidays the faithful are more available and ready to put dates in their diaries. In order to give a start to the year, wouldn't this be a good occasion to institute a feast of the local church, as a symbol of its own existence and communion with all the other catholic churches? Moreover, this would not be a total innovation, because the Jews celebrate the end of September as their new year (rosh ashana) and the church retained something of this in the September Ember Days.

Probably we should go much further than this and try to work out a new policy of liturgical seasons and festivals with a living rhythm of christian celebrations. Life needs rhythms and high and low seasons. A monotonous series of unchanging Sundays is in contradiction with the psychology of individuals and groups. But emergence from this state has several implications.

First we must accept that there are 'ordinary Sundays'. Otherwise how shall we recognise the festivals? We must accept that there should be an ordinary, habitual carrying out of well-known, familiar rites. On these days everyone must rely on his own faith to celebrate the festival of the Spirit. This is one function, and not the least, of the repeated rite, giving free periods when unexpected meanings can arise. The exceptional occasion will strike with all the freshness and surprise of a party or festival. The ordinary rite carries on in its quiet way as an inexhaustible source of light for the watchful heart.

Then on some days the festival bursts upon us. The unusual and extravagant are shown in the rites themselves, the songs, flowers, lights, words, gesture and special ceremonial of the day. This cannot be achieved without preparation and precautions. A festival must be planned and wanted. It consumes or even 'wastes' in a few moments things that have taken hours or days to prepare. Special symbols are kept for it.

It becomes practically impossible to show that it is a festival if the same songs, the same vestments, the same words are used in every assembly as are used on the festival day. Since the Latin chants were abandoned the general mistake has been made – and continues – of using the same vernacular songs on all occasions. Thus we hear 'God is love' or 'Remember Jesus Christ is risen' at weddings, funerals, on any Sunday and . . . at midnight mass. How can this symbolise Easter? This is not waste for the festival but waste of the festival. Of course there are certain excuses: the paucity of the repertoire for festivals; the necessity of using a certain number of songs every Sunday without the luxury of reserving a particular 'Gloria' for Christmas mass.

But this means there are no special songs for festivals. We must have the courage to economise and strictly reserve certain songs for Advent or Lent if we do not want them to lose their colour. If a particular hymn is only sung once a year on Maundy Thursday this hymn then acquires a strong symbolic value. Similar remarks could be made about statues and images. If the same statues are there every Sunday people won't even see the state of Our Lady on Assumption Day. Better a single statue in the sanctuary to symbolise the festival than a permanent museum.

The first thing about a festival is the assembly itself. Festival means an extraordinary assembly. We should not be scandalised to see people in church on that day who never usually come. There have always been such people. But we could also help to make the assembly bigger by a festival policy which, for example, in a parish with several Sunday masses gives special status to one mass on that day to which all are invited. Or even – we are far too timid about it – we could have only the one festival mass.

And shouldn't some festivals be occasions for large gatherings bringing together all the assemblies in a town or deanery in a single place? The place could have symbolic value such as the cathedral, a place of pilgrimage or a very fine church, or else it could be chosen for the occasion and be held in a different church in the area each year. Such gatherings give a more vivid image of the church celebrating a festival, and show the catholic communion at a strength it cannot attain for a parish mass.

Earlier I arued for weekly assemblies with small numbers, as the necessary condition for obtaining a certain style of gathering in the faith. But I do not think this single type of assembly is enough to make people feel the whole mystery of the church. I have already mentioned the value of small groups where the relationship between the members can become very close. But, as I said, these small select groups only ever interest a minority of christians. I also think that large festival assemblies are indispensable. For some they are the only liturgical form that means anything to them. For others they make a change. For all they show a normal aspect of the society of the church, completing the ordinary assembly (and the small groups) by bringing people out of their chapels and particular churches. They are a sign of catholicity.

A policy of rhythms of celebrations should not stop at festivals and ordinary Sundays. In order to avoid a succession of monotonous Sundays it might be a good idea to introduce series, as in the case of Advent, which is a preparation for Christmas, and Lent for Easter. We might in passing question whether six Sundays are not too many for Lent. Isn't it rather a long haul? This depends on the communities. An arrangement of three intensive weeks might be more effective in certain cases, for example. Why not organise analogous series in the long succession of ordinary Sundays? Some churches do so successfully during the months of July and August for the holiday assemblies (two series of three or four Sundays). I am thinking of a preparation time for the 'feast of the new school year' in September or October, preceded by several Sundays to prepare for it. This does not mean it is necessary to upset the *Ordo Missae* and the lectionary. Sometimes just an 'opening' is enough, with a song, a text, a poem, an image . . . which can be brought out better by shortening other elements in the introductory rites rather than the reverse. Then there could be a special reading, a special intention in the common prayer, a reminder during the eucharistic prayer and after communion. What is needed is not the hammering of a particular idea so much as symbolic coherence. Connections between divers elements are mostly made unconsciously rather than by planning.

65

We want to find new ways of allowing the paschal mystery to break into linear time. We must make careful use of signs, from the humble and permanent sign of faith professed and bread shared daily to the dazzling signs of Birth, Life, Breath and the gathering of a countless throng in the visible and invisible festival.

VII

CLERGY MANAGERS AND LAY CON-SUMERS

Never before has there been so much talk about the role of the laity in the church, the adult, responsible laity, and the ministry of the laity. But there would be less talk about it if it in fact existed. This is far from being the case. The management of the church, and particularly of the liturgy, remains largely in the hands of the clergy, that is in fact the priests.

We also hear a great deal about the equality of men and women and the ministry of women. But the government of the church remains exclusively masculine, although taking advantage of the many secondary tasks performed by devoted women.

In these two ways the practice of the church is behind that of the social development of western countries. This is all the more surprising because the New Testament stresses, far beyond anything that yet exists in any society, the dignity of the people of God – the *laos tou Theou*, from which the word 'laity' derives – the equality of women and men in divine daughterhood and sonship in Christ, and every form of responsibility as a service. Do our liturgical assemblies give any proof of this triple revolution?

Some progress has indeed been made. The image of the bishop as a 'prince of the church' and of the priest as the absolute ruler under God of his parish, are regressing. The hierarchical insignia, like military ranks or honorary decorations, which were displayed during church services, are now less ostentatious (although they still partially remain). Nowadays we see women entering the pulpit to read the bible, or at the altar to distribute communion (although the decree from Rome authorising this practice contains the clause: if there are no men to do it). Things move forward slowly and every step forward, instead of being thought of as progress, is regarded officially as a concession regretfully made to contemporary fashion. However, we are only seeking what is right and good. What is good? Let us ask ourselves a few questions.

Let us imagine that the liturgy for the following Sunday mass is being prepared. Is it better for the priest alone to decide on the songs, the texts, the rites, compose the intentions for the common prayer, prepare the sermon? Or wouldn't it be better for those who are going to celebrate together to share in the preparation of the service and even to take charge of it, because it is their celebration? Priests change, assemblies remain. The liturgy does not belong to the priest; it is a 'service of the people' (in both senses: service for the people whose 'servant' God himself became in Jesus Christ, and service of God by his people).

There is agreement, at least I suppose there is, on the principle. But in fact progress in this direction is not very rapid. Some progress has been made by the setting up of liturgical teams where lay people share in the preparation and the conduct of the celebration: leader, readers, choir master, musicians, take part in the choice of songs and the management of the liturgy. Sometimes they prepare the prayer intentions. More rarely, some lay people share in the preparation of the sermon. But this development comes up against a double barrier. Firstly, the lay people in question are a few more committed, devout, and competent among the many. They only commit themselves. Like the priest, they have their own tastes and opinions. From the assembly's point of view they become a new 'clergy'.

Can things be different when particular talents are involved to do particular jobs? There is no point in letting just anyone read from the pulpit, for the sake of 'democracy', or in bringing someone to the microphone who cannot lead the singing properly or makes useless gestures to conduct the assembly. The Word of God and the singing of the assembly require competent service. Public speaking or conducting must be learnt. Only a few members of the community can do it properly. Of course a woman reading from the pulpit or a lay person preaching the sermon has a sign value, just like the modifying of the sharp distinction between sanctuary and nave. It does have some effect thus to modify the image of the assembly which has up till now been too much of a masculine, clerical and hierarchical affair. But we should go much further than this. Although the assembly requires specialist services (the 'ordained' priest who presides over the eucharist, the reader, the bible commentator, who can give a correct ex-egesis, musicians), each of these 'specialists' are at the service of all, and all are responsible for the meaning of the celebration. This is more difficult and goes deeper than the mere provision of services.

Decades of simply 'attending' mass have made the christian people a passive public. Although there are lay people today who claim their share of responsibility, their right to speak and their status of adult in the church, even though some of these offer to 'help' or 'unburden' the priest, in fact there is always a tendency to leave him the last say in the decision-making and often in the carrying out of these decisions. 'It's not for us – we're not competent – we haven't got the time.' These objections are often valid. And let us repeat that it is not primarily a question of specialised services which only the few competent will be able to perform, but of a certain spirit and relationship within the assembly.

Let us take the case of the service of the Word. This requires a good reader to put it across. It requires someone who knows his bible if the text needs explanations. But the service of the Word does not stop there. There are also – and we shall come back to them – prophecy, witness, exhortation, encourage-ment. The priest's sermon partly provides these. But St Paul sees things differently when he writes to the Colossians (3. 16–17): 'Let the Word of Christ dwell in you richly, as you

69

teach and admonish one another in all wisdom, and as you sing psalms and hymns and spiritual songs with thankfulness in your hearts to God.'

All of us in the assembly of believers must bear witness to the Word for one another. We must bring out what each understands, believes, experiences, hopes of it. There is no Word of God – biblical or present today – without the response that people make to it or do not make. The exclusive use of the sermon has given the faithful the idea that this is something to be listened to, like a bible lesson, a theological conference or a pious exhortation. Singing together corrects this image to some extent. But it remains incomplete. My brother in the faith has something to tell me about the good news, and I have something to tell him. One may be suffering for his faith and another may want to tell of the joy he finds in it. One may have learnt from books, another from experience. One may have something to say because he has the simplicity of a child and another because he has endured the cares of this world.

It is together, in sharing the Word and the bread, prayer and decisions, that we form a church. The assembly is also the place to raise questions concerning the life of a community which is trying to live by the gospel: care of the sick (to whom some members of the assembly can take communion and tell them something about the Word proclaimed that day), the unemployed, homeless, or penniless; the political positions that christians should adopt on social conflict, abortion, ecology or the atom bomb; the running of the community, etc. Clearly the voice of the priest alone is not sufficient for all this.

A similar change of outlook – assemblies acquiring the sense of responsibility for themselves and self-government, in communion with other christian assemblies and under the care of the bishop – could lead to a better division of ministries and services in the church. This, as we know, is a matter of urgency for the life of christian assemblies and communities.

Gradually in the course of time all ministries have been concentrated in the priest. At the beginning it was an 'elder', an honourable member of the community (1 Tim. 5. 17) chosen to ensure its cohesion, preside over the eucharist and be the sign of communion with other local churches. As well as the elder there were travelling preachers of the gospel, deacons for the various community services, and then later on, numerous other subsidiary roles (minor orders). When these fell into disuse the priest became missionary, teacher, liturgist, president of the eucharist, head of the community and administrator of its wealth and works. This is no longer suitable. Many young people who want to consecrate themselves to the service of the Kingdom of God do not feel they are called to play all these roles at once. They are hesitant to join the seminary which leads to this type of 'clericalist presbytery'.

There are, fortunately, other possibilities. For each local community to be supplied with the service it needs, people capable of rendering them should be sought from within it. In our modern western society there are plenty of capable christians whose talents are not used. A strong effort has already been made to entrust part of the ministry of catechesis to the laity, mothers and fathers of children and adolescents. There are also quite a few lay people today with the biblical knowledge necessary to explain the scriptures to the assembly. It would be even easier to find lay people, men as well as women, who could take over the running of the liturgy and the community, prayer groups, etc. Finally, to preside over the eucharist in the local 'sub-communities' and the 'Sunday' assemblies we have discussed, the bishop could choose a father who has brought up his children well, as St Paul says, who is respected by all and capable of becoming the symbol of unity by ordination to the priesthood. Moreover, the question of the ordination of women to certain ministries previously confined exclusively to men, is still fortunately an open one in the church.

I realise that already attempts are being made in various dioceses for the setting up of Sunday assemblies without priests. Lay people in the community are prepared to take over the liturgical services of the Word, prayer and song, and communion. And of course such assemblies give rise to a completely new image of a church assembly because they are truly self-governing. They can do much to prepare the way for future developments. But to me they seem but a palliative, an educational transition to a change of attitude. They do not constitute 'the' solution. I realise that in certain newly converted countries, the church insists on local communities without priests to perform the 'catechetical' ministry and several other minor services, because it seems premature to ordain priests or even deacons. But in many of our own communities it would be easy to find christians suitable for ordination to the priesthood and the diaconate. This would be a more normal situation for the life of the church. It must added that these priestless assemblies should not confine themselves to the performance of rites (the easiest part) but should also take care of the other services needed by the local church.

I have just mentioned deacons. It is astonishing that this traditional ministry of the church, restored by Vatican II to its former status, and now conferable on married men, should have raised so little interest in our western countries. I think there are several reasons for this. First, as I have said, in spite of their declared intentions and good will, the laity are accustomed to leave things to the priest. The number of priests among us is still relatively large. Perhaps there are too many priests for things to change very quickly. Then the role of the deacon is not very clear. 'What is a deacon for?' Finally, if a function is already being performed it is hard for people to see what ordination would add. And people are wary of thus increasing the clergy. I note in passing that the Council spoke of the role to be performed by deacons but said nothing of deaconesses, although they used to exist in the church.

I would venture to say that the point of having deacons and deaconesses won't be seen until real christian communities have been restored. Deacons have a service to perform in the life of the christian community. The priest is ordained to be the sign of Christ as the head (*prae-esse*) of the body of the church, particularly in the eucharist. The deacon is ordained for 'service'. It would even be dangerous to ordain deacons in the present state of our predominantly cultic assemblies, because their functions would be purely ritual. The role of the deacon is concerned primarily with the *koinonia*. It is not indispensable for the service of the Word and the cult. But if there are to be deacons they will of course take their part in these too.

This last remark seems to me to apply to all the restorations of lay ministries. It is right that lay people should take part in the liturgical celebration, by welcoming people at the door, taking round the collection box, bringing offerings and giving communion. But if no link is made between these ritual services and the other functions of the assembly, which are the spreading of the Word and mutual help, if the cultic is cut off from preaching the gospel on the one hand and common life on the other, then it is to be feared that the most committed christians will fight shy of these ministries. Because every service involves the whole church: the whole life of the local church and the whole catholic church.

We have remained within the context of the local community assembly and the services it cannot do without. But these local ministries must of course be complemented by ministries at a higher level, covering an area or a diocese. First we may mention the vocation of evangelist, who has given his life to the service of the gospel and preaching, whether he is celibate or not, in religious orders or not. Then there is the work of theologians seeking every possible way of passing on the faith. Then there are those concerned with christian initiation to the extent that this service goes beyond the capacities of the local assemblies. There are also those who devote themselves to all kinds of church administration and other services. At the moment most of these jobs are done by priests. Many of them could be done by the laity. But it is often the financial problem which makes it difficult for them to do these jobs (the cost of serious training, the normal salary of the family breadwinner). Finally, there is the unifying role of the bishop and his helpers (presbyterium). At this level the service becomes a sacramental sign of God's free gift and the apostolic mission coming from Christ.

Perhaps it seems we have come a long way from the liturgy. Not at all. The liturgy is at the heart of the life of community assemblies. But the development of these assemblies is held up

73

for a number of reasons we have mentioned and about which we shall say more, because tasks which could and should be done by members of the community are not. Many of our wishes for assemblies and their celebrations will be in vain if the people of God and their pastors fail in the prophetic gestures of the diaconate and charismata in the church.

Let us listen to St Paul again: 'Having gifts that differ according to the grace given to us, let us use them: if prophecy, in proportion to our faith; if service, in our serving; he who teaches, in his teaching; he who exhorts, in his exhortation; he who contributes, in liberality; he who gives aid, with zeal; he who does acts of mercy, with cheerfulness.' (Rom. 12. 6–8).

VIII

WORD AND WORDS

Almost from one day to the next the catholic liturgy which had previously been celebrated officially only in Latin has been translated into living languages. Of course there had been a long preparation for this. Missals in English and other languages were widespread among the faithful for half a century beforehand. During the celebration itself some efforts were made to get round the rigour of the law: readings were repeated in the vernacular, prayers superimposed, explanations were given during the course of the service. The change of language has been the most spectacular feature of the liturgical reform. It has been done now.

It is almost superfluous to justify the reasons for it. If we speak it is to say something to somebody. To pass on the Good News of salvation in a language not understood by the people is contradictory. To offer the prayers of the assembly in words which have no meaning for those who hear them is to speak in vain. But although the principle cannot be disputed except by the obstinately peevish, the way in which the translation has been done and is now used still causes problems.

In the first place, the translation is of existing texts. In the case of the bible this is necessary and normal. The bible is a word from elsewhere, another time and place. It comes to us in the form of scripture written in other languages, languages of the past. It cannot be re-written even though it must always be freshly interpreted. In order to pass it on, it must be translated. And translated in a way which preserves the spirit of its own, other, language. Believing that the language of the bible could become our immediate language, the language of our time, would empty it of its historical value and of the very truth it reveals to us: God really intervened in our human history. This is the foundation of our faith in God's intervention in our own time. We should therefore translate the bible in a way that can be understood by us today, into our common speech and ways of thinking. But our translation should not obliterate the text's socio-historical context because this is ancient, oriental and agrarian.

In the christian liturgy the bible is the only 'book', the only scripture. All other texts are the living word of the church responding to the revealing Word in prayers of supplication and praise. This Word, which comes to us from another time and place, is taken over by the church, which expands it, comments on it, brings it up to date, rephrases in many ways, in every time and place. Liturgical books have by no means the same status as the bible. It is not self-evident that the prayer of the church should merely be a translation of ancient texts written in Latin. The people praying in church are praying today in a particular place. The liturgy should be *their* prayer. We should remind ourselves of this to avoid misunderstandings and to understand the awkwardness sometimes felt with a faithful translation of several hundred ancient Latin prayers.

However, the work of translation is not therefore invalidated. Firstly, because the church has a 'memory'. Like every other living society its present is partly formed by its past. We learn to pray in the prayers of those who came before us. Moreover, the church is catholic: every age and every culture offers its own response to the Word, enriches the dialogue between God and man, expands our human language of prayer. Why should we deprive ourselves of all this wealth?

But translation has its limitations. It is also right and proper that liturgical assemblies should produce their own hymns and prayers in accordance with their life in Christ, their language, their traditions, their feelings and their own modes of expression. Otherwise the liturgy might still seem archaic and foreign.

We should not exaggerate the problems caused by translations in our celebrations. Translations are not to blame for everything that is held against them. Other aspects of the word seem more important to me now.

The first of these is the verbal inflation in our current celebrations. In the Latin liturgy the quantity of words only troubled those who wanted to follow every single one, if they knew Latin. Otherwise it was a ritual which gave time for each to invent his own approach to God. For the most part the liturgy was sung or 'chanted', which offered a form of expression and communication other than the bare 'meaning of the words'.

The total translation of the liturgical texts into a comprehensible language, and the way in which they are now uttered, have totally changed the ethos of the celebration. From beginning to end words come to us — often through loudspeakers forcing them upon our ears – which make a constant demand upon our minds. Apart from the moments of silence, which do not last long, and the singing, the amount of which varies from one assembly to another, we are bombarded with a continual barrage of 'information': admonitions and introductions, readings, prayers, prayer intentions, sermon, the long monologue of the eucharistic prayer.

This is usually too much to follow, especially for someone who is not familiar with the kind of language used and its subject matter. The effect is of saturation. We feel we need protection from this verbal attack. Some people feel guilty because they are not attentive or receptive enough. The more mystical regret that their minds are constantly engaged, leaving too little place for the heart and contemplation. Others miss the Latin and its 'mystery', especially the silence of the canon: are they so wrong? Some take refuge in their books or let their minds wander.

The question is, what is the best amount of texts and words

to have in the celebration? There is also the problem that the readings and prayers are usually far too fast. We are literate, so we forget that the listening ear assimilates more slowly than the reading eye. We are used to private conversations, the telephone, the wireless and the television (which is addressed to individuals rather than groups), and we have little experience of the 'public' word. Finally, since we are saturated with words by the mass media, advertising, etc., the power of the word has been largely devalued for us.

Apart from the excessive quantity of words in our liturgies, there is the deeper question: the atrophying of the human functions of language. The middle-class person who forms the majority of our congregations speaks to communicate ideas and facts. He controls the expression of his emotions and feelings. He does not shout for joy, cry out in admiration, or scream and curse with rage. He does not recite poetry (he hardly ever even reads it), he does not quote proverbs or pronounce sentences, he gives few orders. Perhaps he is still capable of occasionally saying words of love which communicate a great deal more than their semantic content, chatting with friends just for the sake of chatting and 'being together', telling stories to his children; humming as he walks or works. But these 'speaking words' are much fewer than the 'spoken words' which are useful and 'reasonable'.

But the liturgy needs all the functions of human language. It can and does use words for information. But information is only one aspect of communications. It is not even the most important. At some celebrations you learn nothing new because you already know the readings – for example the gospel of the birth of Christ – and most of the prayers. Likewise when we say 'Lord, have mercy!' or 'Glory be to you Lord!' we are not giving information to others, let alone to God! The word has also the function of making contact. When we say 'Good morning, how are you?' we are not usually thinking about the meaning of the words. But it is a way of showing that we are aware of the other person. The word creates a personal relationship. Likewise when the president says: 'The Lord be with you' and we reply 'And with your spirit', we can of course reflect on the deep meaning of these words. But the act of speaking remains valid even if we don't: it introduces the assembly's celebration by establishing a relationship between the president and the people.

When I cry *Kyrie eleison* or *Alleluia*, I express myself as a sinner asking forgiveness or as a saved person who gives thanks. We should make it clear that the expression does not merely put into words a state or a feeling already there. It brings something into being. By calling 'Forgive me' I confess myself a sinner to God the Saviour, I become aware of myself and become the 'subject' of God's forgiveness. The same goes for thanksgiving in the *alleluia*. The religious historian Van der Leeuw remarks that the religious person never says 'Enough words: let's get on with the actions', because for him word is action.[2]

That is why we repeat the same words in our prayers, the litany, the chorus of a psalm, in meditation. Just as those in love keep repeating 'I love you', because it intensifies their loving relationship, the christian at prayer keeps repeating 'Father, if it is possible . . . listen to me', or naming God with all the names by which he thinks of him: Good, Strong, Most High, Most Near, Most Far, Light, Darkness . . . The word is also a way of influencing others: 'I beg you . . . please', and the way in which I commit myself: 'I believe in you. I count on you.' There is no objective neutrality in the liturgical Word. It is always my life – and others' – with God.

This is why the 'story' in the liturgy is quite different from the narrating of past facts or the repeating of a valueless myth. The story of the creation is the foundation 'myth' of the meaning of my relationship with God. The story of the institution of the eucharist is the Word that gives meaning to the act of sharing the bread and the cup. It is the foundation of my relationship with Christ who died and rose from the dead.

All these human functions of the word are brought out by the special form in which they are used. There is a tone for giving orders (sharp and imperative), or for asking (respectful

2. Cf. La religion dans son essence et ses manifestations, Paris 1948.

and pleading). There is the cry of admiration. There is the saying which gives a treasure of wisdom in a phrase. And finally there are all the forms of poetic language, with its imaginative leaps, images, rhythm and assonance, etc. Here the form itself becomes the meaning.

We lose the chance of restoring all these various functions of language to the liturgy unless we give them a significant form. A psalm which is not said as a poem is no longer a psalm but just an obscure and insipid text. An *alleluia* or an *Amen* which are not 'acclaimed' become a mere collective mutter. A preface which is not a high lyrical proclamation is no longer 'eucharistic'.

And if the word regains its active, affective, expressive, imaginative values creative of meaning and commitment, from the meditative murmur to full-throated song, then the 'informational' weight is lifted. Space is made for the heart and the unutterable groans of the Spirit. The words themselves regain their power and savour.

Among the acts of speaking during the celebration, we must of course think of the sermon. During the course of the mass it is an important item. It is usually longer than any other element in the mass, song or prayer, longer even than the eucharistic prayer. This type of word is interesting because it introduces 'direct speaking' to the assembly, in the sense that it is formally addressed to them, whereas the rest of the prayers, songs and readings are indirect and addressed to God or others. The sermon should thus be an easy form of the word. On the whole people listen to it.

Homily originally meant 'familiar conversation'. Let us admit that this is not the usual effect of the sermon. Firstly, because usually only one person speaks. This makes it more like a conference, or lesson. Then, the tone and style are usually didactic or at least a type of intellectual reflection. Of course the catechetical task (to instruct and to moralise) must be done. We are not questioning the necessity of catechesis but whether the sermon, during Sunday Mass, is always the best place for it.

Although the sermon must explain the meaning of a bible

reading or a mystery in the life of Christ, and although it cannot neglect the moral consequences to be drawn from the gospel of the day, this is not the 'point' of it. The primary function of the homily is prophecy, in the New Testament sense, that is to say the proclamation of God's intervention in Jesus Christ. 'Today this happens for me, for you, for us.' God speaks to us through the response of faith that believers give to Christ's call, as they have heard, understood and experienced it. This word is also an example and encouragement given to the rest of the assembly. There is no reason why this prophecy should not be a story, a parable, a meditation, a poem or a song. If the priest remains the 'moderator' of these interventions, they can come from different people. It is wearisome always to hear the same witness. Hasn't everyone his own witness to bear so that all can see the great work of the Word which cures, frees, and transforms this world? I have already mentioned the importance of the word 'going round' the assembly. The homily as a conversation also involves new practices which are now being tried, like discussing in small groups, prepared talks by members of the assembly, audio-visual aids.

I shall return in another chapter to certain rules governing oral communication – now restored to the liturgy – and to the relationship between the living Word and a fixed or improvised formulation. With regard to symbolism I shall insist on the importance of form in any words seeking to be meaningful. Let me end this chapter by the reminder that for us christians the word is not just speaking. The Word is first and foremost a person, by the living communication of God in Jesus Christ. Thence it becomes action: the act by which the church confesses its faith, commits itself to its saviour, proclaims the coming of salvation and communes with him it praises. Because by the Word 'we continually offer up a sacrifice of praise to God, that is, the fruit of lips that acknowledge his name' (Heb. 13.15).

IX

MUSIC AND SONG

In the contemporary change in the liturgy music, as well as Latin, has been a sore point. Once the church was split over the date of Easter or unleavened bread. Now groups are being formed to sing Gregorian chant. There are clashes over the use of the guitar and other instruments. The newspapers go to town from time to time on the debasement of music in the catholic church.

As always in these upheavals, which are socio-cultural as well as religious, what is apparent is only the tip of the iceberg. We might find it surprising that music has suddenly become so important, when the christian cult can be celebrated entirely without singing or music (proclamation of the word, prayer, the Lord's supper, baptism). Likewise we might be tempted to smile at the battles over Latin, since the gospel should be preached in every language and everyone has always first prayed to God in his mother tongue. But this would be to forget that 'manifestation' is also part of man's being, both individual and social. The way in which we dress, talk, behave, sing or don't sing is part of ourselves, for ourselves and for others – and for God in worship.

In order to understand the present state of liturgical music and song, we must first make a few points clear.

Within a few years the repertory of ritual song has been completely transformed. The corpus of traditional or canonical melodies which grew gradually over the centuries and was condensed in the *Graduale romanum* suddenly became redundant with the adoption of modern languages in the catholic liturgy. These books lie unused in sacristy cupboards or organ consoles. The many 'ordinaries' of the mass for several voices, which were the basis of the choral repertory, have been forgotten. We do still hear the *Missa de Angelis* or the Credo III in some places. But already the young no longer know them. Except in the occasional monastery and a few select assemblies, the great majority of songs used today are recently-composed vernacular ones. This rapid and enormous changeover arose from a background of slower and deeper developments previously affecting liturgical song. First there was what could be called a change from the 'ritual' to the 'aesthetic'.

Liturgical music has always had ritual status. Until modern times a distinction was made between *cantus eccesliasticus* (rite) and *ars musica* (art). The former was part of the ceremony: chanting psalms, the *Kyrie* the *Alleluia*, bell-ringing were not primarily an exercise in the art of music but ritual practices. This state of affairs remained even when developments in Western music brought polyphony and 'sung masses' to enrich the ceremonies with the culture of the time.

However, modern subjectivity has laid more stress on the aesthetic aspect of music. Church music is now expected to be 'art'. It must be performed by artists, whereas formerly it was the business of the clergy. The restoration of Gregorian chant at the end of the nineteenth century was in this context. All church singing is now thought of as 'music'. It is judged by the aesthetic standards by which the art of music is judged in that particular culture as a whole. This is what Pius X meant in 1903 when he said that liturgical singing is a 'true art'. This aesthetic conception of church music was imposed within and by the cultivated classes. By the time the repertoire was changed, it had become general. This fact helps us to understand certain current distortions, about which more later.

The changeover from ritual to aesthetic in accordance with modern subjectivity went side by side with a development of the concept of sacred music. For a long time *musica sacra* was nothing more than the music used by the church in its cult. Its language, style and technique might be the same as those used in other music of the period (e.g. a motet or madrigal by Palestrina and a liturgical or profane cantata by J. S. Bach). Its ritual use was what made it *sacra*. With the increasing secularisation of society, the church began to seek originality in its own music and produce its own aesthetics. At the end of the nineteenth century there was sacred music which was 'solemn', inspired by archaic models (Gregorian and Palestrinian), just as Neo-Roman and Neo-Gothic architecture was 'sacred' in contrast to contemporary secular architecture. St Pius X was quick to canonise this idea of religious feeling. When the first collections of French hymns appeared for liturgical use after the second world war, they were neomodal, neo-folkloric and neo-classical. They still are for the most part.

After 1966 the first so-called 'rhythmic' or 'swung' hymns were sung in churches; they no longer imitated archaic models but contemporary pop and American jazz, and were accused of aesthetic decadence and desacralisation. But this did not prevent them spreading, thanks to the mass media, to a large number of assemblies.

But in all this where is the true music of our time, the music that concerns the educated musicians of today? Apart from some contemporary organ music played in some churches, there is a great lack. This is an obvious anomaly. It has been said often that if the church had consulted 'great musicians' in its liturgical reform, this would not have happened. But that is a gross over-simplification of the problem. It goes without saying that the church ought to express itself musically in the musical language of our time. Aren't modern churches at last being built in the modern architectural style? But on the one hand we still have to discover what is 'the musical language of our time', and on the other, whether the point of view of modern composers is compatible with the needs of our current liturgical celebration.

The liturgical reform took as one of its first principles the active sharing of the faithful in the ritual action, which includes the singing. If this means not just listening to the music but taking part in the singing, it follows that the music must be 'singable' by the average member of the congregation. What music are most French people capable of singing today? Very little besides the classical major-minor modes, 'the musical mother tongue of the west', with a few modal variations inherited from Gregorian chant and folksong, or taken over from popular music. This is what most people know and thus must be recognised as 'the musical language of today' for the majority of people. All the rest belongs to an educated and scholarly minority. It consists of works which are more or less performable by ordinary choirs and instrumentalists, which the public at our liturgies are more or less willing to listen to. These are the cultural limits within which we must seek acceptable ritual music.

In such an awkward situation the most astonishing thing is that the assemblies do sing! They do, and much more than they did a quarter of a century ago. Then nearly all the masses celebrated on Sundays, particularly in towns, were 'low masses', that is without singing. The singing at high mass was generally mostly done by the choir. The Gregorian movement did succeed, with brave and persistent efforts, in getting some assemblies to join in the singing of the ordinary of the mass. But this never became general. Then came the 'read masses with singing in the vernacular'. But except for local efforts with ancient popular hymns the people did not do much singing.

Today the opposite is true. There is singing at most Sunday masses, especially in towns, where it is easier to find leaders of the congregation. And the singing is essentially by the congregation. If we think about it this is a surprising sociological phenomenon.

The change was not brought about by a change in the general culture, but by the ideology of the liturgical renewal: 'The ideal form of community participation in the celebration is singing.' When I said this twenty-five years ago I was asked: 'How can you expect people to sing during the liturgy who no longer sing in their daily lives? Singing can never be a genuine expression of their prayer if it does not come naturally to them. The modern bourgeois does not sing. He goes to the opera, to a concert or listens to the wireless. The worker does not sing at his work. Rural folksong is dead. Singing in church is bound to be artificial and formal. In fact yet another ritualism.'

However, there has begun to be singing in our churches. The ideology of the liturgies would no doubt have been insufficient to cause this change, if people hadn't also discovered the value of singing at prayer by experience, just as you experience movement by walking. Moreover, I don't think the contemporary renewal of singing outside church has had much to do with it. This is singing mostly by professional soloists who are listened to. It is not an example of singing together. I would say the same for the renewal of choral singing in France; although this has been important it has only affected a minority. But I do think the current de-freezing in our society of modes of expression in general has had a certain sociological influence, as has the growth of the 'sound' industries (records, television, cinema, radio, cheaper musical instruments). However, I still think the current phenomenon of singing in liturgical assemblies is original. It is a product of the vitality of the assemblies or at least of their organisers.

If this brief analysis is right, we should not be surprised that church singing comes into conflict with several accepted social and religious ideas: the traditional image of sacred music, cultural standards in aesthetics and the art of music, the current trend of contemporary music. However, this singing is probably connected with a development in society whereby the individual is seeking new forms of expression and communication, where the arts are re-discovering forgotten functions, and prayer is re-creating bodily and psychosomatic behaviour which had fallen into disuse. I am thinking in particular, in music, of the workshops where 'making music' is more important than the music made, where music is made for the pleasure of making it, not for a 'public' and even less for the critics, but to be together musically with others. These efforts are connected in several ways with what cultic music should never have ceased to be trying to do.

The traditional ritual image of the 'sung mass' created an effect of 'distance', with its fixed chants for the Ordinary (*Kyrie, Gloria* etc.), variable ones for the Proper (Introit, Gradual, etc.) and the chants for the celebrant and ministers (dialogue, preface, etc.). The Vatican II reform turned back to ancient models to try to make the singing fit the needs of the assembly better. It kept the existing points for singing as constitutive rites, with the further aim of safeguarding the 'treasury of sacred music' (Gregorian chant and classical polyphony). Then it completed the series with the acclamation of the anamnesis, the universal prayer, the chanting of the central part of the anaphora, and possibly a post-communion hymn. It relaxed the old system a little by allowing certain texts to be sung or spoken, other texts which were not going to be sung to be omitted (introit, alleluia, offertory, communion), and making it possible to integrate the *Kyrie* with the confession.

In fact the former model of the sung Latin mass was modified to such an extent that it no longer exists. Most of the chanting has been abolished, especially of readings and prayers. A way of speaking whose first concern is to communicate the content of the text was preferred to the sacral image of stylised chanting. In the dialogues such as 'The Lord be with you' and the acclamations like 'Amen, Alleluia, Glory be to thee Lord Jesus', there is a wavering between singing and speaking because it is impossible to revive a shout or real proclamation, singing sounds too conventional and speaking too flat.

As for the songs themselves there is also some wavering. The *antiphonarium missae* gave each bit of the proper a Latin text which did not vary, and 'consecrated' music, (Gregorian). Thus we had *Gaudete* Sunday or *Reminiscere* Sunday, each called after its own special introit. Today at every mass we seek in the repertory of songs and chants available the ones which are suitable for this or that particular assembly. The repetitive aspect of the chanted rite, and the cumulative emotional force of particular chants attached to particular feasts, no longer exists. There remain the fixed pieces. By insisting on the function each song or chant has in the course of the rite, the reform rightly smashed the image of a musically unified 'ordinary' (the 'mass' as a musical genre). The true force of the rites took over. The fundamental musical model of the 'mass' which governed a whole epoch in the liturgy and the history of music, which also retrospectively influenced the Vatican Gregorian *Kyriale* at the beginning of this century, and even produced dozens of 'masses in French' after Vatican II, is definitely over (in the sense that it can now only be done artificially).

In spite of all these pitfalls, an ideal is proposed: a mass containing twelve bits of singing, not counting the dialogues and brief exclamations. This musical programme is quite capable of execution, but few assemblies manage it all. If they do, what is the result? Suppose that the mass lasts one hour. Take away the time for readings, sermon, prayers proper, silences – let us say thirty-five minutes. This leaves an average of two minutes for each song. This causes problems.

A brief song can of course be an intense moment, for example in the acclamation of the anamnesis. But can an accumulation of brief songs give true musical satisfaction, give the assembly the chance to enter into the common singing, and produce the effects that music should: linger over the words, touch the heart, lay open the mystery, give the feeling of festive enjoyment? Isn't such quantity mere consumerism, using a large number of songs each Sunday, necessarily partly the same ones, which end up losing all their savour – supposing they had any in the first place? Aren't people going to get bored and the people right who say 'there are too many songs at mass', too many words, too many ritual activities, and not enough contemplation and silence? And how can you make a whole of so many disparate little bits, how can you create the rhythm of a celebration which goes forward in confidence and majesty?

This leads us to the question of the function of ritual and singing, which was a key question in the liturgical reform. For each rite the question was asked: what effect do we hope to produce by offering this sign? For example, is the entry hymn an accompaniment to the music for the entry of the celebrant (the organ alone would do), or is it to introduce the key text for the mass of the day (it could be read out or written up on a board), or is it for the assembly to come into church with an act of celebration? Or is the *Kyrie* an invocation to Christ the Lord, a pure *laus canora*, a litany of supplication, or a penitential act? And so on. The procedure was to go through the service point by point, seeking the function of each bit of music. There was little thought about the connections and the totality. Was the question asked, for example, if it was more meaningful for the 'opening' to have three bits of singing (introit, *Kyrie* and *Gloria*) or just one? Or whether the unity of the eucharistic prayer was best served by four brief moments of singing (initial dialogue, *Sanctus*, Anamensis, doxology) separated by long monologues? Meaningfulness comes from the totality, not from each element alone.

Furthermore, the functions examined were those that were manifest, explicit and intended. There was little investigation of those that were latent, hidden, diffuse, although these are often more important. When I go into a church during the opening hymn, what is it that attracts or repels me? Not just the tune and the text of the hymn but also the sound as a whole in given acoustic conditions, the arrangement of the singers, whether they are enjoying or embarrassed by their singing, the style lively or dreary, the length of the hymn . . . In other words whether the rite functions satisfactorily or not depends as much on *how* it is done as on its mere doing. This involves the people taking part, how they feel, their culture, their attitudes, their conscious and unconscious reactions. It is not enough for the psalm to be in responsorial form for there to be an effective 'response' by the assembly to the word.

Another point connected with the manifest or latent functions of singing which some of the faithful feel strongly about is the fact that the assembly does sing but what is the aesthetic value of their singing? 'Yes we sing, well or badly, badly rather than well. It doesn't sound good. And what they give us

89

to sing is ugly. It was quite different when we had Gregorian chant!'

I'd like to make a few remarks on this point. First of all, it is easy to idealise the past and memories are short. If we had recordings of masses from thirty years back we would find that indeed Gregorian chant is beautiful but what they made of it often was not; for a musician it was often extremely painful. But at that time it was part of the rites . . . In fact I am surprised by the absence of critical sense among our faithful, even the educated, about what they sing in church, even more surprised than by the objection quoted above, which usually comes from the odd musician or people who are conservative rather than true music lovers. Likes and dislikes on this subject arise from many other causes than the objective consideration of what is sung. The context in which the song is sung (devoit or boring liturgy, enthusiastic or embarrassed participation) often has more influence on people's reactions than the song itself. Moreover, except in the case of a soloist or a choir to whom the congregation listens, there is no audience, strictly speaking, in the assembly but only participants (whether they actually sing or not). When you are really taking part in the singing it becomes impossible to judge the total effect of the song.

The 'aesthetics' of a liturgical song is thus not only to do with the quality of the text and the music, but with the whole ethos of the celebration of which this song is a part. Thus a very simple tune can be dismissed as worthless if taken in isolation but make a marvellous contribution to the spirit and beauty of the celebration, whereas a great work which is too difficult or badly done can wreck it. The final question is, what aesthetics are we talking about in the liturgy? In other words, what value do we put on what is made manifest (the realities of the faith), and what in that which manifests them?

I think the claim that we must 'pray with beauty' does not get us very far. The success of this saying, which Camille Bellaigue picked up from Pope Pius X, lies in its very ambivalence. It continues to lead musicians and music-lovers astray. I'd like to recommend a quite different approach by suggesting the values I think music and singing offer the celebration – although in doing so I am avoiding the question of certain currently held notions about art, beauty and music.

i) The first service that music and singing can offer the liturgy is to give it a 'tool for celebration'. When an assembly joins voices in an act of celebration it needs material: words, rhythms, sounds. For example, to ratify with a meaningful Amen the prayer that has been said in its name. Two notes (or even just one) and an elementary rhythm are enough. Is this art? Is it music? Is it beautiful? I don't know. But it brings something essential into existence which previously did not exist. To find the right form do we need a 'great musician'? It would be like asking a great writer how to answer 'yes' or 'no' to a proposal of marriage! Or, at a more complicated level, there is the singing of a hymn. In this case the art of the poet who wrote the verses and of the composer who made the tune is of course involved. But a hymn is primarily a shared means of praying rather than a literary or musical 'work'. That is to say, it can be 'outside' the stylistic categories of any school or aesthetic trend of the time. What would be 'faults' in a literary anthology or at a concert aren't necessarily so in a liturgical action.

But we cannot stay at this elementary operational level in the liturgy – although it is always the most important in the singing of psalms, acclamations and simple prayers like the Our Father. We also need music for festivals. Then we expect something more sumptuous: good tunes, moving harmonies, catching rhythms and a sound to fill the space. We can't expect this each time for every occasion. But on certain important days, flat, feeble tunes would be a disappointment. On these days we need polyphony, instruments, larger works. People would also like to recognise them, hear well-known music which symbolises the feast for them, as in the past, for instance, did the *Exultet* at Easter.

People expect to see the connection between the music and the festival easily, otherwise they are disappointed. This music for a 'festival for all' cannot be taken from repertoires that some would find archaic and others avant-garde. There will be a preference for classical and romantic old favourites (just as there is at weddings), and – as these periods produced no liturgical compositions in the vernacular – neo-classical and neo-romantic pieces brought up to date. If the service done by music to the liturgy stopped there – and it too often does – the complaints of true artists or of contemplative types regretting the superiority of Gregorian chant would be justified. But I am convinced that music can bring something else very specific to the celebration. Just as images ought to make us contemplate the invisible, so should music enable us to hear the unheard. I see two ways, among others, of attaining this. The first lies in the sound signals which we have not heard before, which astonish us, wrench us out of the familiar or the academic and turn our minds toward new spaces of the spirit. Couldn't contemporary music do this? Of course we would not expect these sounds to be produced by the assembly as such, but in it and for it by people with the talent to produce them, or the gift of inventing them. But are we capable of finding a place for such talents and gifts?

The second special service could be by the kind of music not necessarily new and surprising in its language, not necessarily too difficult to perform, but so suited to what it is celebrating that it would be an inexhaustible source of prayer, meaning and feeling. A very simple and pure symbol, like the water of baptism, the candle flame, the broken bread. A music that was not full of itself but the bearer of silence and worship as Mary bore the incarnate Word.

I often hear people ask: 'Which way is liturgical music going? Is the neo-tonal and the neo-modal going to go on? Shall we be submerged by the current trend towards popular or folk song? Is there any hope of integrating serious contemporary music into our services?' I can't answer all these questions. But I can make some suggestions about the future.

In the celebration the music will depend on the development of the celebrating assemblies. We already find that small groups don't sing much. They'd rather listen to a record or one of their members accompanying himself with a guitar. But great festival assemblies cannot do without music and singing.

In fact music is often composed with these occasions in mind. As for the ordinary Sunday assemblies, it is difficult to predict what they will be like in the future. But we can already note certain points.

First, that performance and style are more important than the actual repertory. The liturgy is a working symbolic action, not the representation of a finished work. The way in which it is done and the meaningfulness of a given practice are more important than the songs or the rites themselves. This is even truer of the music than of the texts and the ritual gestures. There is too much emphasis on works, language, and 'codes' in general, but not enough on the importance of performance, on the musical act as a manifestation of what is happening, as a visible sign of the invisible.

I am also afraid of an excessive 'consumption' of songs during the liturgy, and this from two points of view. Firstly, we try to make too much of it, in the sense that as soon as we open out mouths we expect the result to be musical, festive, enjoyable, moving . . . The result is often exhausting and pretentious. As it is impossible to keep this up twelve times during one mass and at every mass, as we lack the courage to go for simplicity and the capacity to make it all rich and beautiful, we end up with a succession of songs which sound both dreary and complicated. Who will have the courage shamelessly to go for simplicity, without trying to emulate the concert or the popular song backed by an orchestra? This does not, as we have said, exclude the possibility of a choir or an instrumentalist occasionally producing something more elaborate.

Moreover, we sing too much, in the sense that there are too many insignificant little bits of singing and not enough real moments of song which require both time and intensity. I have taken part in celebrations of the mass where instead of the prescribed twelve songs, there were only four: a work introducing the community into the common symbolic action; a psalm as a living anamnesis of the word proclaimed; a eucharistic prayer uniting in a great song of praise – the high point of the mass – the memorial of the Lord's supper and his pascal sacrifice; finally a hymn of thanksgiving after the communion. This mass was one of the most musical, prayerful and praising I have ever taken part in. So who dares do less in order to mean more?

Finally, we should free ourselves from too narrow a conception of music which restricts us within a cultural field of sounds. There are an infinity of cries, acclamations, proclamations, chants, pluri-melodies, instrumental sounds and noises that the liturgy could use and welcome – practices known to other cultures which are outside our range. I consider that electronic support has been beneficial. The microphone makes it possible to use several different tones of voice; loudspeakers enable us to hear instruments we otherwise would not: the guitar, lute, harpsichord, zither . . . and the production of original sounds. We could go much further in this.

But we should not forget that the human voice and the human body remain the most important means of expression and communication of both sound and rhythm (including dance). What we make of it in our liturgies is still elementary, or even primitive and crude. To improve we need techniques, but they are not sufficient of themselves. The first thing necessary is the intense life of the spirit in a body of believers celebrating together.

This has been the longest chapter in the book. And there is still so much to be said! The reason is not primarily that music and song have taken up most of my energies in my previous work on the liturgy. The fact is that they bring out in an exemplary manner nearly all the problems involved in celebrating the mass today as a common symbolic action. Music and song have always developed furthest in the liturgy of the past. They could be the touchstone of our capacity to re-create for tomorrow a living and meaningful liturgy.

X

SYMBOLS THAT SYMBOLISE

'We should not be surprised that the symbols in our liturgy do not speak to our contemporaries. They are nearly all borrowed from nature, whereas we live in an industrialised world, centred on people and machines. The symbols also come to us from very distant cultures: the Semitic culture of the bible; the Greco-Roman culture of the Mediterranean; the culture of the Franco-Germanic court, etc. It is high time we gave the liturgy modern symbols if we want it to be intelligible today.'

This is a summary of proposals I have heard or read for the last twenty years. They show two things. First, that the role of symbols is recognised as important in the liturgy. Secondly, that the way symbolism functions is generally misunderstood and that over-simple notions on it are all too easily entertained.

Because the liturgy is concerned with the realities of the faith which are beyond immediate experience, it operates wholly in the realm of signs and symbols, in 'sacraments' and 'mysteries'. That is to say that nothing in the liturgy exists invisibly without being manifested and, contrariwise, nothing is manifested (in principle) that does not concern the realities of the faith. Moreover, no one can enter into an immediate relationship with God. As Pseudo-Denis says, his divine light is always refracted through the veils of this our world (our bodies, the natural world, our cultures). Ritual activity is not concerned with producing purely 'worldly' effects (of this world), but the coming of the Kingdom. Thus in the liturgy we do not eat only to feed our bodies; we do not sing only to make music; we do not speak only to teach and to learn; we do not pray only to restore our psychic equilibrium. The liturgy is a parabolic type of activity (which throws us aside), metaphorical (which takes us somewhere else), allegorical (which speaks of something else) and symbolic (which brings together and makes connections).

This is always a very complex operation. There is always the risk of over-simplifying the theory so much that its application becomes false. Here are some examples taken from current discussions on the liturgy.

Symbols are spoken of as things: the symbol of light, of water, of bread. We cannot completely avoid this simplifying language, which is based on the fact that there always is a visible object which 'signifies'. But we must not be deceived by it. The symbol is never a thing. It is a human operation. We use light, water or bread to symbolise illumination, immersion or nutrition and the shared meal. If we find that the symbolism does not work, we will not necessarily solve the problem by changing the 'thing' which symbolises, for example by exchanging candles for electric lights or baptismal fonts for a bath tub, or the host for a cake. There are no objects which are of themselves symbolic. They can only be made so, either in a situation where they acquire a special meaning for me, or in a particular culture where they have this for the group. So no one can simply 'make' symbols by manipulating objects. We can only support actions which have the chance of becoming symbolic.

Sign and symbol are confused and the latter reduced to the former. With a sign there is a signifier which refers to something signified, and vice versa. If I read or hear 'horse' I think of the animal designated by this name; if I see the animal I think 'horse'. The same goes for mathematical signs like +, −, =. Each is a reversible pair, message-meaning. The ideal of the sign of communication is that it should be une-

96

quivocal: that the message produces the intended meaning and not another.

It is different with the symbol. If I see a lake, I may be afraid of falling in and drowning or I may want to dive in and bathe, or both at once. The lake can make me think of coolness, calm, or life (fish and plants) or destruction (if it breaks its banks) and many other things. A symbolising object can lead to all sorts of other realities, which are often themselves symbolic. Thus the reversibility of the message-meaning pair is never assured. If I think of life or death, I do not necessarily think of water, perhaps I think of animals, or flowers . . . One of the consequences of this is that it is impossible strictly to predict or to programme the effects, 'meanings', connotations of a symbolic operation. Thus I can share in the Lord's supper every Sunday and always find new meanings for the sharing of the bread or for 'This is my body'. These new meanings come partly from my wishes, my experiences of life, my knowledge, my situation. But it is neither certain – nor indispensable – that every Sunday when I go to communion I think of 'eternal life', 'resurrection' or 'unity' of the body of Christ.

It is therefore a mistake to think that 'the' meaning of a symbol can be explained. Strictly speaking it means nothing. It is not like a word whose meaning can be looked up in the dictionary. It is an inexhaustible source of possible new meanings. Hence its richness. It is the chance offered to the faith of the believer in the liturgical celebration. A consequence connected with this is that the director of the rites cannot expect to produce a particular effect with a particular meaning by any particular symbol. If he does not get the effect he had in mind it is not necessarily the fault of the rite, which has probably produced other effects he is unaware of and which may be more interesting for certain members of the congregation than the effect he intended.

A third frequent reduction of symbolism is to confine it to the order of knowledge. But the liturgy, like all symbolic activity, is not concerned only with knowledge, it is also pragmatic. It is not only an -ology (as in theology) but also an -urgy (as in dramaturgy). The symbol (and the sacrament) manifest and operate both at once. It produces meaning but also feeling. It affects self-awareness, wishes and freedom. It invites you to take a stance. This is much more important in the symbol than knowledge, especially in matters of faith.

It is a serious mistake to judge the impact of a symbol from what you have explicitly understood by it, and even worse from what you can put into words about it. For this reason many symbols were removed from the liturgy because they were thought to be inexplicable, incomprehensible to people today, when they clearly still had living force. I have often noticed, for example, how the faithful like the censing of the altar at the beginning of the mass. I asked what meaning it had for them. 'I don't know,' they reply. I perservered, remarking that it was an oriental custom absent from our culture; that often people felt nothing about it, and that the sickly smell of our imported incense in fact upset some people (including the singers) . . . 'Perhaps, but I like it.' Likewise if someone asked me why I was moved by a particular passage of Bach, what could I say, except talk about musical theory and style, which are neither the cause nor the explanation for what I feel? The relationship of the message to my reaction is not 'cause and effect'. The mechanism is infinitely more complex and richer, because it is creative.

I leave this analysis there because I do not intend to give a theory of symbolism, but to consider some more practical problems concerning symbolism in the liturgy. In the first place, it is false to say that people today are out of touch with the world of symbols because their mind only functions on the cognitive level, of technical language and utilitarian or moral behaviour.

It is often true that their conscious speech only uses this register. But a more careful observation of their behaviour shows that symbols are still important in their lives, although they may often be unconscious. No one falls in love without symbolising the object of his love. He calls her all sorts of names ('my sweet', 'my little one', 'my treasure'), which create a certain relationship. And no one invents or creates without symbolically projecting what he seeks. Only if we come to the liturgy without hopes or fears, without longings or hunger, will the rites symbolise nothing and remain indifferent or curious 'objects'. Moreover, people who are not accustomed to poetic, artistic or musical language or symbolic acts among their means of expression and communication find the liturgy like a foreign country whose customs and language are strange to them.

In considering symbolism we must not forget the importance of cultural factors. Someone coming into church and hearing 'Behold the Lamb of God who takes away the sin of the world' without knowing anything of the biblical and christian context of the phrase, would probably be bewildered at its meaning and wonder how he should respond to such a statement. However, it would be false to say that 'that means nothing to him'. People often say this and thereby only reveal their ignorance of psychology. No one receives a stimulus without responding; someone who hears this phrase can perfectly grasp some of the symbolism from the word 'lamb'. And let us note in passing that it is not at all necessary that this person should have seen a lamb in the flesh. He might think for example of 'gentle as a lamb' (a simile current in our cultural usage rather than taken from empirical experience). But he could not think, if he had not heard, of the Lamb Victorious spoken of by Daniel and the Apocalypse, an image which is absent from our culture. He could not, if he did not know the story of John the Baptist pointing to Jesus, refer this phrase to Christ, who alone gives it meaning for christians. A moderately well-educated christian might think about John the Baptist's phrase in terms of 'He who was led to the slaughter like a lamb' because he knows this bit of the bible, but not of the Victorious lamb because he does not know this part. But this would not be a sufficient reason for omitting the phrase. Firstly because memories of pictures can add the missing image of the Victorious Lamb to the concept. And above all because the presence of the 'unexplained figure' is the very condition of symbolism.

If we only wanted to keep words and gestures in the liturgy whose meaning was perfectly understood, explicit and their denotation plain, then all symbolism and ritual would be futile. This is what those people think for whom the signs are only the outward, perhaps irritating, show of clear ideas, the only object of faith. In this case there would be no more point in having sacraments because we would have come to the end of history. But this is not the case. Figures and symbols are still there to give meaning to the constant newness of what life produces for our faith. They are always the meaning to seek, the risk to run, the promise to keep, the covenant to renew.

Our explanatory and moralising liturgy needs figures whose very mystery is our hope, metaphors that surprise us and lead us on (where?), poetry which 'means nothing' but which makes us think and imagine (what?), music which does not give us information but which moves us (how?), and the gesture which commits us (to what and to whom)? Thus and only thus can we go to meet Him-who-comes as the utterly new, Him who would never have restricted us within an ideology or possessed us by a moral code.

After having stressed the point that the symbolising 'thing' is not the 'cause' of a meaning which it may or may not have (because its effects depend on the individual, his wishes, his culture and his freedom), we must now stress the opposite point: the form is determinant in the act of symbolising. There is no poetry without a poetic, no music without an intentional use of sounds, no rite without breaking away from purely ordinary utilitarian behaviour. The difference from the ordinary in the symbol is always shown at the level of form. It is this 'difference' from the ordinary that gives it its special possibilities of meaning. From this I draw two conclusions.

In the first place, a liturgy with living symbols will never succeed unless care is taken about the forms. If we try to be nothing but clear and comprehensible in our words (explanatory and informative function of language), nothing but efficient and practical in our acts and behaviour (identical factory-made discs for hosts), nothing but effective in the common singing (always simple tunes which everyone can immediately pick up) and so on, we give symbols less chance of working. In fact we make it impossible. In many ancient songs there suddenly comes the line you don't understand, the difficult note, the break in the rhythm. Why is it these songs in particular that last and are treasured, and others not?

The reaction against the hieratic or grandiloquent ceremonialism of a certain type of 'solemn' liturgy, the desire to have only 'authentic' (?) signs, the Council's wish to make the rites understandable, the resistance by a certain contemporary attitude to the haziness of symbols and poetry ('It's not serious', 'it's not logical'), and other reasons brought about a fury of spring cleaning, throwing out 'rubbish', and even 'deritualisation'. People now prefer the kitchen table for the eucharist, the common glass, ordinary red wine and bread. But perhaps we have not sufficiently realised that this behaviour may have seemed 'significant' to those who advocated it because it was a 'break-away' from a ritualism which had become too familiar – that is to say that this anti-ritualism became highly ritual and this apparent desacralisation reawakened the sense of the sacred. But the effect of such a 'surprise break' quickly wears off. Soon these groups start bringing out a table cloth, a few flowers, a goblet.

In these small group liturgies their fairly strong faith has less need of complicated symbols for the sacred. But in a 'public' assembly where the group is not so tightly knit, it is more necessary for the forms to suggest the 'beyond' by their 'extraordinariness'. That is why we need altars which are not just dining-room tables, unless it is an exceptionally beautiful table which shocks us into awareness. This is why the priest, who is also 'other' than himself, wears vestments. But in all this there are no a-priori rules. We have to find the right balance and enough of the unfamiliar for the symbolism to work and not leave people simply immersed in their ordinary experience. But it must not be so hieratic or esoteric that it puts people off. This balance varies of course with the cultural level of the congregation, and with the festive importance of the day.

If the form suggests symbols we must have confidence in it, even if it seems to have little effect. I am thinking primarily of the constitutive elements of the sacraments of the liturgy.

101

At the time when frequent communion was reintroduced, first outside mass and then within the mass, the mass was very little like a meal, which was in fact the fundamental symbol chosen by Jesus for the eucharist. Symbolism was effected differently: real presence (individual); nourishment by the divine life; expiatory sacrifice. But when 'house' liturgies were introduced in small groups, the sharing of the bread and the common cup automatically regained its deep meaning. The people who took part said so, even if they found it hard to put into words. That is to say that the very act of sharing a ritual meal (the difference from a meal with friends even on a special occasion remained plain) reawakened meanings that dozens of attendances at mass had not. I said earlier that something similar also occurred in the singing of liturgical assemblies. I think the same could be done for the act of immersion, the fundamental symbol of baptism. A thesis on the sociology of religion written at Louvain showed that today the meanings perceived in baptism almost ignore the symbolism of the bath: release from original sin, divine sonship or joining the church are what come first to people's minds. At most the image of water 'washing away' sin is barely mentioned. Even death and resurrection in Christ is a doctrine learnt and believed without any direct connection with the sacramental act.

Why be surprised at this if we continue to be satisfied with pouring a few drops of water on the head of the person being baptised? And what would happen if we put more trust in the form of 'baptism' (dipping), the act of immersion and coming out of the water, with all the strangeness involved in such public behaviour and the ritual nudity involved? The change in practice could bring about a change in its symbolism. It would bring out Paul's being buried with Jesus and risen with him. But we are afraid of the unusual. Is it because it could lead to mystification? Certainly. But it could also lead to mystical faith.

Having confidence in the power of the symbolism of our rites is a condition *sine qua non* for the future success of our liturgy. It's true that this is asking much of both priests and faithful. The whole liturgical reform was based on active and conscious participation, that is to say on the intelligibility of the rites and the results we are aware of them having on us. Priests must therefore take care to make sure that anything said or done has really 'got across', been effectively communicated and received. The faithful for their part are ill at ease if they have not 'understood', and they remain inclined to prefer rites whose effects they can consciously evaluate. But what priest can forsee the symbolic effects of a rite, for example when he reads a poem or breaks the bread?

Who knows clearly – for example when he goes to communion or when he sings – what happens interiorly to his faith? The liturgy is always a risk. The true rite creates an empty space, into which the Other can come. But unfortunately we are afraid of risking a bible reading thought to be difficult or an unusual gesture like the kiss of peace. Unless it is merely lack of awareness or laziness, as in the case of the sharing of the cup at the eucharist: will we be able to go on much longer hearing the Lord say to us at every mass: 'Take all of you and drink', and still not drink?

Should we seek 'new symbols'? 'Modern' symbols? Perhaps. But where are they? Who has them? Shouldn't we rather put our trust in the human realities that Jesus and the church took from our bodies and souls, from nature and culture together, to signify God coming to make a covenant with man? These signs and sacraments, because they are a history, our history, will not cease to have constantly fresh meaning today and in all times, places, cultures, individual or collective situations in the light of the sign of Jonas, the single symbolic key given to men in Christ who died and rose from the dead, until He comes.

XI

SPONTANEITY, CREATIVITY

Spontaneity, creativity, authenticity, expression, communication, festival . . . There is a whole vocabulary of the liturgical renewal as celebration (the word celebration itself is part of it), a whole group of words whose evocative power seems all the greater the vaguer their meaning. This vocabulary is quite close to that of May '68 in France, and to that of the late sixties generally in other western countries. Nobody doubts that it seeks human values glimpsed and wanted. The fact that this comes out in society as well as in the christian assembly shows that it is not just a question of ritual forms but of human life as a whole. This deserves our attention.

There is no point in going back over the dissatisfaction felt with the paralysing rigidity the Roman liturgy had reached on the eve of Vatican II. I also learnt to celebrate mass in those days (in 1951), putting my thumbs under my armpits to say the prayers. When I bowed over the altar I made a cross on its edge by drawing back my little finger under my ring finger . . . I was also taught that in the liturgy anything that was not prescribed (written in the book) was forbidden. I won't pretend that this prevented me from praying. For every human gesture form and meaning can be learnt; and inner freedom can only be won by overcoming external constraints. But my body could have given me other ways of praying which I could then neither copy nor discover. We were also taught to celebrate without caring about anybody. This was the period of the first 'wrong way round masses', as Paul Claudel called them (altars facing the people), and dialogue masses. How could we celebrate without taking any notice of the people? How could we truly greet them with hands that gave the impression we were drawing out a concertina?

All that now seems very far off. But reminding ourselves of it may help us to understand how priests and faithful of a certain age were badly prepared to make use of a freedom so suddenly offered. And are the younger people any better prepared? The problem is not to stop doing what we did in the past, but to find a true expression of the mystery we experienced, body and soul, in the liturgy. Wanting does not mean getting.

It is right and good to seek for spontaneous individual and collective behaviour in the celebration. True spontaneity is the commitment of our whole being freely expressing its own deep truth in its behaviour – and discovering it *hic et nunc by* its behaviour. Such harmony is rare, a moment of grace. For most of the time we have an obscure desire to commit ourselves which finds no adequate expression. So we have to borrow already tried forms of behaviour to try and find the truth that has escaped us. It would be an illusion to think we could always be spontaneous.

This illusion lies behind many liturgies which try to be spontaneous on principle. Because the proposed texts and rites do not exactly express what we feel and think we experience, we substitute improvisation in word and act. What then happens? Only immediately available expressions in content and form come out. But, except in rare moments, the immediately available is usually poor and superficial. The improvised prayer falls back into the same clichés, the same ideas, in banal and dreary word forms. The improvised tune makes use of known tunes and messes them about. The improvised gesture is vague, dependent upon the whim of the moment and usually familiar in form. The truth expressed thus remains superficial, just as in prescribed modes of expression it may be a mere façade.

Moreover, when we have to go from individual expression –

which can succeed – to collective expression, this type of spontaneity is full of pitfalls. How is it possible to improvise a song or a text or a movement together? Some 'model' must be offered and a collective game played. And there are no games without rules.

Why is spontaneity which tries to express the truth of the moment by what happens to come out at that moment so feeble? It is not through lack of will to be true but of means to show it. True spontaneity comes from a long inner growth in its expression. It is like the pianist who has to practice a Mozart sonata for hours, days, months, until he has identified with it. Then he can interpret it as if it really came out of himself. Or someone who has prayed and meditated long and often on a psalm and one day finds the right expression of its deep meaning.

The instituted rite may seem to be against immediate spontaneity, which claims to create its forms of expression freely and on the spot. But it is not against a deeper spontaneity. On the contrary, it allows what has not yet been expressed to come out within its confines. Rite makes us work on ourselves. It takes us out of ourselves, 'elsewhere', so that we can then come back to ourselves. It takes us out of the 'ego' to give a chance to the 'self' which we did not know and did not yet exist.

Besides the temptation to indulge in 'spontaneism' there is the current tendency to literalness, which only allows the expression in the liturgy of what has already been experienced, understood and felt by members of the assembly. This is often formulated thus: 'Liturgy should celebrate life.' This is an ambiguous formula. Its truth depends on the meaning given to the word 'life'. If this life is reduced to what people have experienced, the realities and plans they are conscious of, if the celebration is intended to celebrate this life to the exclusion of all other whose expression would be 'inauthentic', then liturgy means celebrating yourself. We celebrate ourselves in a 'review'. This is the opposite of liturgy, which manifests what is to come, what we are not yet but are called to be, a great people – including everyone besides ourselves – waiting for liberation. What is to come is more authentic than what has already happened. In this sense the symbolic rite, which anticipates, is truer than experience. We can and should say that liturgy celebrates life, man alive, but the life God offers us in Jesus Christ, and man alive in the fulness of this gift.

This had to be learnt. The mystical life in Christ offered by sacraments and eschatological faith under the veil of signs, in the liturgy, is the fruit of a slow growth. Immediate religious experience is closer to our contemporaries than the slow progress of the rite. Religious experience brings something that is understood, felt and enacted in the celebration, and finds visible expression in daily life. It is on this level of experience that liturgies are called 'successful' (participation, atmosphere, warmth, beauty), or a failure. Adolescents and many adults need this experiential aspect of the liturgy. They 'feel at home'. But rite involves going into the dark. We must risk the adventure of faith in the name of hope.

Celebration as symbolic action must therefore find a balance between pure religious experience (which is pre-liturgical) and a bare ceremonial of ritual 'figures' which would have no impact on the assembly. This involves 'creativity'. I will not discuss the meaning of this neologism. I think it means this: life never exactly repeats itself. It creates its forms from models within itself and is constantly adapting. If liturgy is life, it should behave in the same way and constantly adapt its forms. Even if the rite is laid down, it is like an inner model of a meaningful act whose form must constantly be reinvented or modified. Even if the rite is by nature 'repetitive' it is never pure repetition. At the level of the realities of the faith, the liturgy is always newness, new covenant, paschal renewal. So shouldn't something of this newness be shown at the level of the signs? New being and new appearance are inseparable.

This principle involves the whole liturgy. It was the basis of the Vatican II reform which wanted, as the Constitution on the Liturgy says, 'to adapt to the needs of our time those institutions that are subject to change' (Const. Lit. 1). It concerns the vast question of the relationship between the cult and the culture, which is being asked in every country in the world. But it also concerns the detail of the functioning of the rites. I will give a precise example of this almost daily reality: the prayers that the celebrant says in the name of the assembly.

Let us take the three prayers of the mass and the eucharistic prayer. They used to be said in Latin, whispered or out loud, and functioned as the ritual figure of 'prayers offered to God' without any immediate link between their saying by the priest and the understanding of them by the faithful. When they were translated and even broadcast through loudspeakers, they regained their nature as prayers addressed to God but said so that the assembly could hear them and associate with them. What do celebrants make of them? Some simply read the official translations from the book. Others use these texts but edit them. Others use different prayers that they have found in books or have themselves re-written. Others improvise.

From the point of view of the listening faithful, the differences noticed are not usually the above-mentioned: whether it is an official or unofficial text, whether the text is taken literally or modified. Oral communication, restored to the liturgy after more than a thousand years of a dead language and the reign of the 'book', brings out two important aspects: what the faithful expect or do not expect; the dominant character of prayer as a reading of an existing text or as actual praying together.

In the case of the prayers of the mass, the congregation hear a text whose content and formulation they do not usually know in advance, unless they have read it or are reading it in a missal for the faithful, which is rare. They therefore do not realise whether the text is official or not. That is the priest's point of view. But they are aware of three things.

The first is the tone of the speaker: he either reads a text which is obviously not his, or he expresses himself as if he were composing the prayer on the spot. The first tone sets a distance between the celebrant and his hearers. This 'distance' is right and proper in the case of a bible reading (even if it is read in a lively manner) because it corresponds to the truth of the thing, but it is regrettable in a prayer which is supposed to be the prayer of the church assembled here and now. The second tone can be used for any text whether it is written, re-written or improvised, provided the celebrant makes it his own and thus expresses it. Here the newness (creativity) shows, less in the formulation than in the tone of voice.

The hearers are also aware of a second thing: the style and conceptual schema of the words, in other words the 'oral model'. No communication is possible unless the hearer has the same language categories as the speaker. All story-tellers know this by instinct, and oral literatures show this clearly. There are procedures which are really models to ensure that communication takes place. The Roman prayer invented the structure: 'God . . ., who . . ., now make . . ., through Christ'. This structure, which comes from the bible and which corresponds to the usual structure we use for petitions: 'Because you . . ., will you . . .', can still function. But if the prayer is said in the vernacular, the Latin word order must be surrendered. Syntactic structures must be found which are familiar to the listeners, otherwise they will not follow. Even if the prayer is wholly improvised, it cannot do without formal models. The important thing here is less to sound up to date than to avoid archaism or the esoteric (some modern prayers are too stylised or literary and do not go down well).

Finally, the listeners are aware of the content and connotations of the words of the prayers. Certainly many of the very abstract and non-temporal propositions of a number of Roman prayers, even if they are very beautiful (such as 'since your grace is our sole hope keep us under your constant protection'), have less chance of being taken in by the assembly than formulations with more images, closer to daily life. Finding the right formulation can help the assembly to grasp that this is its own prayer, here and now.

The eucharistic prayer is a different case, because it is a fixed prayer in the sense that part of its content never varies and the faithful know these few formulations well. They expect it to go in a certain way with given words. Some celebrants read. The result is even worse than in the other prayers, where at least there is the novelty of change. A conventional tone for known formulae does not bring anything to life. To escape this others use quite different prayers. But this is not automatically an improvement. In the first place it is important not to give the impression that these are 'read' either. Furthermore, too great a departure from the known models risks losing the benefit, for the hearers, of a familiar procedure which eases communication and makes it easier actually to pray.

Isn't the solution to be found in the practice of public prayer according to the laws of oral communication used before the era of the written text? We often hear it said that the celebrants in the first three centuries of the church 'improvised'. But this word gives a wrong impression if we take it to mean that they invented everything, form and content, extempore. In fact they used received models on given traditional themes. This is exactly what Hippolytus of Rome did (3rd cent.) in his anaphora, which has become our eucharistic prayer II. I understood better what was entailed when I read K. Hruby[3] on the rules of prayer in the synagogue. At the moment of the *Shemone Esre* (long prayers containing 18 intentions, analogous to our universal prayer), first there must be a silence, during which the faithful say these prayers in their hearts. This presupposes a traditional formulation known by all. During this time the person who is going to say the prayer aloud considers how to say it. He is absolutely forbidden to read it. He must always recite it. He says nothing other than the eighteen predetermined intentions. But he must prepare the verbal form.

This behaviour is both faithful to 'tradition' and careful to make it come alive each time for the listeners. I have not yet found a better suggestion. Within the framework of received

---

3. Cf. K. Hruby, 'L'action de graces dans la liturgie juive', in B. Boote, D. Webbs, R. G. Coquin et. al. *Eucharisties d'Orient et d'Occident*, Paris: Cerf (coll. 'Lex Orandi', 46), vol. I, 1970, p. 44 ff.

prayers (thus with a known structure), making use of traditional formulae (which act as firm reference points and whose phrases can always produce new meanings), certain phrases are inserted, using verbal equivalents, soberly recalling the word announced beforehand during the mass, discreetly mentioning the situation of the assembly. Thus the word comes alive again, communication with the assembly is renewed, the prayer is for today. In doing this you have not invented a 'new eucharistic prayer', but celebrated for today, for a particular assembly, the eucharist of the church.

I have spent quite a long time on this example to show that between ritual fixity and absolute creativity of forms – two blind alleys between which many of our current celebrations waver – there are ways which are both traditional and alive, supple and sure. We have so many elementary things to relearn before we can be simple and true! It remains to see that in order to make the liturgy truthful and alive, all the cards are not in the hands of the agents of the celebration. Their personal means of expression and communication are often fairly limited. And furthermore, a collective symbolic action requires that the assembled christians should have a minimum of means of expression common to them all. Where are they to find them but in their common humanity and the culture that formed them?

In times and places where the society's culture was fairly homogeneous, the church was able, without question, to use anything in its liturgy which it found available and suitable to the christian cult: poetic and musical forms, makers of respect, signs of festival, etc. (This is true at least for the near-eastern church, and was so for the western church until a certain date. From the seventeenth century onwards, in mission lands, this principle could no longer be applied, as was shown in the sad 'quarrel over rites' in the far east.) But today it is not as easy as that in our contemporary western world where folklore is dead and cultures broken down. In many assemblies it is difficult to tell what is the common culture of the faithful. We can find certain common languages and codes which enable us to speak, sing, draw (but alas, not to dance).

But what meaning and values do we thus convey? What type of music, painting, poetry should we use in the liturgy? The fashionable mass media's? The culture of an élite avant-garde? The culture of an ecclesiastical tradition which has become archaic?

In the past when we celebrated mass, everything was laid down in advance, or almost everything: codes, messages, context of interpretation. It was only the situation that changed, and the ministers. Today every celebration is a problem. Its (visible) success depends to a great extent on the flair, competence and gifts of a celebrant or organising team.

This means that today celebrating assemblies must find their own culture – and pass it on to one another by exchange and osmosis – the equivalent of a common culture (or rather 'sub-culture', that is to say the culture belonging to a group within a larger culture). There are realities to be signified in the liturgy for which we do not find adequate signifiers in our secular culture: words, prayer attitudes, ways of speaking or singing. When the former models of celebration no longer function, they must be re-created, often without expecting to find equivalents in secular social life.

Does this mean that christian assemblies must accept an apartness from the world around them? This seems to go against a whole missionary trend which tries to conform its behaviour to the world in which it finds itself in order to make the church's presence felt. As Aristaeus said in the second century: 'The christians are not distinguished in society by a special way of life.' But the daily life of a christian in the world is one thing, and the assembly of christians amongst themselves is another. They are celebrating what is theirs: their expectation of the Kingdom to come in the Spirit renewing the face of the earth. I do not think this is possible without a certain apartness.

If what is revealed to us is 'other', its manifestation will show this otherness. Not that we should have esoteric rites. On the contrary, there is nothing commoner than the christian symbols: water, bread, oil, simple words, easy songs, human gestures like bowing, shaking hands, eating and drinking. St Augustine said that the christian cult, unlike the pagan cults which were complicated and incomprehensible, had few signs (*sacramenta*), simple, accessible to all, and transparent. Every time the liturgy has strayed from this ideal it has not improved. Even after Vatican II there still remains much that is too complicated, heavy and difficult. But it is not in its symbols, vocabulary and gestures that the liturgy stands apart. It is in its way of doing things, its style.

I am convinced that there is a christian style of celebration. A way of celebrating the God of Jesus Christ in the Holy Spirit. I do not mean by style particularity in the sense that there was the Roman style or the baroque style but in the sense that 'the style is the man'. The christian liturgical style is paschal man in Christ. St Augustine described him by a word that is difficult to translate: *castitas*. There must be both reserve and openness, respect and simplicity, confident joy, everything I find in an Autun capital, a Gregorian melody, in the prayer of St Francis, certain monastic choirs singing psalms, certain of the faithful in the way they bring the bread to the altar. Tradition with its biblical roots used another word which we now hardly dare use: unction or annointment. In spite of the word, if we think about it, this annointing of biblical times does perhaps suggest what the true spontaneity of the celebrating believer should be: an expression impregnated by the Spirit of freedom and love; a body through which the light and love of the risen Christ already shines; a people already saved in hope, who can follow the Lamb wherever he goes.

XII

THE TRANSPARENCY OF THE GOSPEL

'For consider your call, brethren; not many of you were wise
according to worldly standards, not many were powerful, not
many were of noble birth; but God chose what is foolish in the
world to shame the wise.' (1 Cor. 1. 26–7).

This is how Paul saw the Corinth community, and he re-
joiced in it. Since then the western church has passed through
a thousand years of power and prestige. Political power governing states; intellectual power in its schools, theologians and
philosophers; power of patronage for artists, architects, pain-
ters, sculptors, musicians; financial power of a property
holder; social power of the clergy, etc. The liturgical
ceremonies bear the marks of this historical situation, which
we cannot judge without putting it in its socio-religious context. For example, there are the insignia of the bishops and
clergy, the court ceremonial, the most prestigious monuments
in the city where all the arts flourish, teaching *ex cathedra*,
funeral and wedding pomp.

In our secularised post-christian society the relationship
between the church and the world has become more complex.
Although the church, as at Vatican II, is seeking a return to
the gospel, it still bears the heavy weight of its cultural and
sociological heritage which obscures this sign. This is also true
in ritual, sacramental and liturgical life.

How can we make baptism not simply, as it still is for a

114

large number of French people, a rite of introduction into society, but the sign of entry into the church of Jesus Christ who died and rose from the dead? How can we make first communion the high point of christian initiation, and not just a family festival for a rite of passage from childhood to adolescence, ending the period of catechism classes and often the practice of religion altogether? How can we make marriage not only the religious solemnising of a human celebration (although also holy in itself) but the sign of the union between Christ and the church?

Two pastoral tendencies are now in conflict – as always – on these serious matters which involve both the appearance and the nature of the church. The first, the more radical, calls for the purification of the signs of the faith and a return to the gospel. It concludes that there should be fewer baptisms, solemn communions, weddings, but that they should be more meaningful and truly evangelical. This is the only way the church can go back to the gospel and its special role as defined by Vatican II: 'to be the sacrament, that is to say both the sign and the means of close union with God and the unity of the whole human race.[4]

The second tendency is more aware of the mixed values which are always present in sacramental initiations. Opposing religion and faith, or profane holiness with christian holiness, is just ideology. Devaluing 'religion' to give greater value to 'faith' is an illusion. It is also a pedagogical error. Because in every man there is *homo religiosus* and a natural sense of the sacred which is a preparation for the gospel. To despise this is to despise human nature. And if the christian church is for many the only easily accessible religion to honour this reaching out towards the divine, why should it refuse to do what it recognises as legitimate for non-christian religions?[5]

Let us note that this second tendency does not advocate simply carrying on with current sacramental practice. Both want change, one a clean break, the other continuity.

4. Vatican Council II Dogmatic Constitution, *Lumen Gentium* n. 1.
5. Cf. Vatican Council II, Dogmatic Constitution *Lumen Gentium*, n. 16.

A similar oscillation can be found in the ordinary practice of the liturgy. On the one hand the need is felt for detachment from a style of celebration weighed down by too much wealth, whether inherited from the past or imported from the 'world'. Christian rites should go back to the 'castitas' spoken of by St Augustine. We have noted this in passing when we were discussing church buildings, ceremonial, music, certain 'visions of the world' sometimes reflected in the style or conceptual framework of the prayers. If signs are to be transparent, in faith and in art, they must be economical.

And, contrariwise, we must not forget that signs are for men, all men. They are to help their faith. We must therefore take care to find signs that work. Enlightened, highly motivated and educated believers can make do with few signs, which are simple but evoke biblical and ecclesiastical history. However, the majority of believers need to be led towards the word and the sacrament by more immediately obvious signs, numerous and varied: sacred atmosphere of the place where the cult is celebrated, music, lights, beautiful forms, paintings, flowers, songs, warm words – in other words by a certain ritual richness. When we celebrate the liturgy it is not a question of choosing between élitism and demagogy. We must seek, for the assembly in question, what I'd call a transparency of the gospel. And this is of another order.

Pastoral work during the last few decades, which has shown such vitality in so many fields (lay apostolate, catechesis, biblical renewal, liturgical movement, workers' mission, theological reflection . . .), has been unable to avoid a certain élitism because its contributors were clergy and intellectuals.

In the field of the liturgy alone, the pre-conciliar movement, though wanting the participation of the people, found its most convinced and effective supporters among an enlightened minority: historians, theologians, biblical scholars, priests who were aware of what was at stake. Thanks to a few determined priests, it affected a small number of laity in a few parishes. They offered intense instruction on the liturgy and the bible, they forced the assemblies to sing and made a few ceremonial alterations. Some of the faithful who realised its values for faith and prayer, responded. But the renewal did not come from the base. When Vatican II called for liturgical reform, even though the ground had been prepared in certain countries, this was still a reform imposed from above. It is hard to see how things could have been otherwise. Before the Council pioneers were needed. And for the conciliar reform to take effect in all countries, it had to be imposed.

But the enterprise still bears the marks of its origins. The example of the paschal vigil is a telling one. While it was still being celebrated on Holy Saturday morning, as a deformed remnant of ancient practices which had become foreign to the christian people, liturgical historians reminded us that it should be a night vigil, the 'mother of all vigils', the supreme festival for christians, the privileged moment for baptism. Then several prophetic groups of enlightened believers, with the help of archaeology, restored this vigil. With the support of the liturgical, biblical and theological renewal – Louis Bouyer published *Le Mystère Paschal* in 1945 – the idea spread. Some parishes celebrated the vigil as a 'para-liturgy' until Pius XII, even before Vatican II, restored the night of Easter in 1951. The conciliar reform took this over. But what exactly had it acquired?

Twenty years' practice of the paschal vigil have not succeeded in making it the festive assembly *par excellence* of the christian people. Attendance varies from place to place. Sometimes the numbers are large, sometimes quite small. At any rate it only affects an élite of the faithful. The others 'do their Easter duty' at another mass. It is a difficult celebration to manage. Although the initial rite of the new fire has been well received, what follows is more problematic: a packet of biblical readings and songs which are abbreviated as much as possible; a baptismal festival where baptism only takes place occasionally (especially of infants); a eucharist like any other. Hardly anyone risks the nocturnal vigil and the paschal eucharist before dawn. In many English parishes the vigil itself is celebrated midway through Holy Saturday evening rather than at 11 p.m.

And yet the signs offered are of great value, highly

traditional, biblical and sacramental. In themselves they are not more difficult than others – those of Good Friday for example. So why the difficulty? Among other causes – including the fact that many people are away for the Easter holidays, as we have already mentioned – it seems the signs do not work well because the restoration was too 'high-brow', élitist and based on a knowledge of archaeology. The major signs: light, the announcement of Easter, the baptismal bath, the festive meal, do not seem to me to be the trouble. Rather it is the general tone of the celebration and the way the elements are put together.

As it is the greatest of all christian festivals, where is the break, the 'excess', if we make do with a simple mass (with only a slightly longer introduction) celebrated at the end of the evening? Where is the night vigil waiting for the resurrection? And this at a time when young people – and not so young – are quite happy to have parties lasting far into the night? Moreover, who complains about the midnight mass at Christmas, which wouldn't be the same if it wasn't at midnight? And shouldn't the festival eucharist be followed by fraternal agapes in the joy of the risen Christ? Isn't it the day of days when the biblical word ought to be shared, meditated on in silence, resung in all kinds of forms, illustrated in symbolic images? The day when all should share in the cup? Indeed the festival derives from the message of Easter. But the celebration of it cannot just come from the book containing the prayers and the rites. It must come first of all from the assembly who welcome the Good News of Christ risen. Our assemblies have not yet really made it their feast.

In due proportion analogical reflections could be made for the Sunday Mass. Isn't its evangelical force to some extent weakened by an excess of signs? Some people have discovered the fresh power of the most essential signs at the Sunday eucharist if they are reduced to their most elementary form: a word which calls for response, a prayer expressing the hope of the group, a communion of shared bread. A single reading from the bible, a few prayers, few or no songs, a meal in its simplest form and a prayer of thanksgiving were enough. Why in the Sunday assembly do the same signs fail, when they should have greater force?

Apart from the effects of having a small group (personal relationships, simplicity of ritual, absence of formal roles – except that of the priest – strong bond between the members) which cannot be the same in an open assembly, we may still wonder whether an overloaded ritual does not partly hide what it should be revealing.

For example, does the bible sequence: Old Testament – Psalm – Epistle – Gospel, which is supposed to show the historical breadth of revelation both in its unity and variety, constitute a digestible meal? If these readings are not already familiar to the assembly, they produce a flood of phrases rushing over them, not the two-edged sword of the Word of God penetrating the marrow of their bones. And the simple actions of the Lord who blessed the bread, giving thanks, broke it and gave it – that is 'what' we must do 'in memory of him' – are enveloped in a series of over-complex actions. In particular, wouldn't the prayer of thanksgiving stand out more if it were not immediately preceded and followed by a series of other prayers, which are indeed venerable, but less essential? And isn't the opening of the celebration overloaded and formal with three distinct songs and two different prayers? Doesn't everything that separates the eucharistic prayer from communion (except for the Our Father) weaken the connection between the breaking of the bread and the invitation to eat and drink?

All in all, aren't there too many songs, too many prayers scattered here and there which slow down the pace of the Word given and received, the bread and the cup offered and taken? I don't want to argue for a lack of signs. The aim is the opposite one of making these signs as significant as possible.

But how? I see things as follows. The fundamental evangelical signs – the Word proclaimed, simple and confident prayer, the bread and the cup shared in thanksgiving in the name of Jesus – have been gradually overloaded in other socio-cultural and religious contexts with many attendant signs, whose aim was to make them stand out more plainly.

119

This was a normal and even indispensable operation. Not because the mass or number of symbols make them more strongly symbolic, but because the multiplicity of the relationships between them produce new meanings. However, the attendant signs, which are more spectacular and more transitory, always have a tendency in the history of rites to overlay the fundamental, humbler and stabler signs. The ones that were added end up covering what they should illustrate. Thus the sacred silence of the canon took over the anamnesis of the paschal mystery, the adoration of the real presence at the major elevation became more important than the offering to the Father. This has been put right. But is it enough? Doesn't the eucharistic prayer sound more like a monologue by the priest than a great high prayer of the whole assembly to the Father? Don't we often have to wait for the moment of communion in the mass to realise that the sign is a meal? If we want the major signs of the christian cult to come to the fore again, and be re-enriched by all that would make them expressive for us today, shouldn't we have the courage to detach them from all the superfluities that weaken them? The Vatican II reform tried to do this and partly succeeded. But it was easier for it to prune things than to give a living form to the essential elements.

Only particular assemblies can do that, within a specific culture, by their language, their music and their behaviour: rites of courtesy, respect, festival, prayer, the meal, clothing. The reform kept what it could from tradition because it was sanctioned by the religious culture of past generations. But what gospel transparency have these treasures from the prayer books, music and rituals of the past for our assemblies today?

Because they found that the liturgy, even translated and restored, was still a screen for many of the faithful of good will, some priests have tried to express themselves in a more immediate and simple way: common, even colloquial language in the announcements and prayers; popular music for the singing; maximum reduction of ceremonial (vestments, processions, movements, prayer gestures), electric lights, standard ritual objects. In short, anything that might be found esoteric was avoided. Scripture of course was kept. But when possible, simplified translations were used.

Does this bring about a great transparency of signs? It makes the celebration easier to understand, immediate participation easier, more familiar surroundings. But it can also result in a liturgy which is flat, one-dimensional, deprived of the multiplicity of signs and symbols in which nothing acts as a sign because they have all been taken away. The assembly turns back to itself. In the prayers, for example, I've often noticed that the language quickly becomes intellectual, ponderous or moralising because it is deprived of images. For how can we pass from the visible to the invisible, without images, except in the abstract? How, if everything is said, can we suggest anything? In the rites, the ceremonial people wanted to avoid was quickly replaced by a few material operations, which became almost irritating. In the last resort one almost wonders why there is a cup and bread, because one has clearly said what one believes and has to do as christians.

These highly conscious liturgies are usually unimaginative and uninventive from the point of view of celebration. They fear utopia, the eschatologising alienation, the ritualist failure of commitment. Isn't this turning into a gnosis in which the sacrament merely illustrates a knowledge and a morality? The transparency of the signs also disappears if the glass is too dark, if behind the window there is no luminous world to contemplate. We are on the dark side – the darkness of faith. The signs are not there to reflect our own light. Neither are they themselves a source of light. They refract into our bodily and worldly existence a light which comes from elsewhere. They are not there to be seen but to see by. They are there to open our eyes to other things. Neither are the rites 'what must be done for God'. They call man to freedom. They call him elsewhere: to die and rise again in Christ, to pass over with him to the Father.

We may well wonder if the liturgy today is not more preoccupied with itself than with the Kingdom it proclaims – like some of our contemporaries who are so anxious to find their identities that they forget to live. It has been said that the modern church is too self-conscious of its 'visibility', its 'image', the way it looks to the unbelieving world. It should care more about its Lord, proclaim his Word, offer the signs of his resurrection, show forth the charity of his Spirit – just as He in this world was a 'call' to the Father. How much the more should the liturgy, which is addressed to believers and those seeking faith, be preoccupied with Him whose living mystery it celebrates: his liberating gospel which 'came to you not only in word, but also in power and in the Holy Spirit and with full conviction' (1 Thess. 1.5); his saving actions which forgive and bring us back to life; his love poured into our hearts by the Spirit. Like Jesus, the liturgy is a 'call' (mass = missa), a gift to the Father.

We should listen again and again to the strong words of the prophet:

I hate, I despise your feasts,
and I take no delight in your solemn assemblies.
Even though you offer me your burnt offerings and cereal offerings,
I will not accept them,
and the peace offerings of your fatted beasts
I will not look upon.
Take away from me the noise of your songs;
to the melody of your harps I will not listen.
But let justice roll down like waters,
and righteousness like an ever-flowing stream.

(Amos 5. 21–4)

Jesus did not weaken this message but repeated it in all its force 'Go and learn what this means, "I desire mercy, and not sacrifice" ' (Mt. 9. 13).

And St Paul described the only true christian cult thus: 'I appeal to you therefore, brethren, by the mercies of God, to present your bodies as a living sacrifice, holy and acceptable to God, which is your spiritual worship' (Rom. 12. 1). The liturgy will remain crucified like the Lord whose glory it celebrates. Solemnities are vain, words are empty, music a

122

waste of time, prayer useless and rites nothing but lies, if they are not transfigured by justice and mercy.

But where man's longing meets the Spirit of God and is transformed by it, everything becomes of priceless value to him:

'and wine to gladden the heart of man,
oil to make his face shine,
and bread to strengthen man's heart'

(Ps. 103. 15)

from the 'this' that is Christ's body and the New Covenant in his blood to the simplest of words spoken lovingly. There will always be people to say of the liturgy what Judas said of the anointing at Bethany: 'Why this waste? For this ointment might have been sold for a large sum and given to the poor' (Mt. 26. 8–9). But there will always be those who answer like David when his wife reproached him for leaping for joy before the ark and making himself ridiculous: 'I will make merry before the Lord' (2 Sam. 6. 21).